AF216988

isb GmbH - Systemische Professionalität
Institut für systemische Beratung, Wiesloch, Germany
www.isb-w.eu

isb-handbook

© 2021 Bernd Schmid

Author: Bernd Schmid

Cover, Illustrations: Bettina Gentner, isb-GmbH

Publishing & print: tredition GmbH, Halenreie 40-44,
22359 Hamburg, Germany

ISBN: 978-3-347-28426-5 (Paperback)
           978-3-347-28427-2 (e-Book)

isb | handbook -

systemic professionalism

Creating Shared Realities

by Bernd Schmid 2019

Dr. phil. Bernd Schmid (born 1946)

is the founder and leading figure of isb GmbH Wiesloch (since 1984) and the Schmid Foundation (since 2011). He has worked internationally as a speaker, learning and professional culture developer, and as an entrepreneur and founder of initiatives and associations. Today, he provides his expertise in organizational development and coaching as a mentor and concept developer at the intersection of profit and nonprofit entrepreneurship.

Schmid is, among other things, an honorary member of the Systemic Society and honorary chairman of the executive committee of the German Federal Coaching Association. He is a recipient of the 2007 Eric Berne Memorial Award from the International TA Association ITAA, the 1988 Science Award from the European TA Association EATA, and the 2014 Life Achievement Award from the continuing education industry. In 2017 award for his life achievement from the German Society for Transactional Analysis DGTA.

Numerous essays on personal and professional topics can be found at

www.isb-w.eu/campus/de/schrift/Blogarchiv-von-Bernd-Schmid-0000SY0812D

Additional publications for free download, as well as videos, are available at www.isb-w.eu/campus/de and www.youtube.com/user/ISBlearning.

Copying, use and redistribution of all materials accessible via the isb website is permitted and encouraged, provided the source is acknowledged.

Contents

Foreword

This book is for quite advanced professionals who are experienced in the field of organizations, having had some education in dealing with roles, structures, projects, markets, as well as taking responsibility and delivering services. It offers an overview over almost 40 years of development at the isb and introduces into the isb way of understanding and dealing with professionalism, organizational processes and development as well as questions of consulting and entrepreneurship.

Nevertheless, beginners may still be fascinated by the isb systemic approaches and get inspiring perspectives for further learning. However, they might miss step-by-step explanations of how things can be done and more examples illustrating isb-ideas. Browsing is facilitated by the gray background of key phrases.

Advanced professionals using these framing descriptions will discover a wealth of descriptions bringing their own experience and reasoning to a point. They may also gain surprising insights, which they can immediately relate to situations they experience within their field. Thus, they may feel reassured and eventually re-evaluate their way of developing ideas and start doing things differently. In brief, this book can help professionals reexamine their point of view, their services and their cultural mission.

You are invited to use one or the other isb-approaches for dialogues and studying with colleagues and customers. Due to the isb policy all further material is free for use. More than 5,000 professionals are actually sharing the isb alumni-network, including representatives of many major corporations in Germany. These networkers, internal corporate employees (2/3) and self-employed, external professionals (1/3) have usually participated in extra-occupational courses at isb for two years and are now working together in peer groups and on projects in many regions and internationally. They exchange insights, practical proceedings, hints and job opportunities. Many of them call the isb their professional home.

Further material to this handbook and each Chapter is provided free on the isb-campus. An instruction in using this material for your own work can be found at the end of this book.

If you are interested in further studying the isb approaches, you are welcome to visit isb-website www.isb-w.eu/en

Join seminars or organize something like a workshop or sharing session locally yourself. There is a lot of material in English and isb runs international platforms for dialogue and co-developing.

My thanks go to

Anandan Geethan and Anuradha Kannan for co-operating in seminars in India and for writing an initial book (Schmid, Geethan 2015) together based on parts of this material.

Rosemary Napper who organized seminars in Oxford, UK and

Renato Morandi who organized a seminar and Coaching-conference in Porto Alegre, Brazil, offering the opportunity to produce videos in English.

Markus Schwemmle and his task force, who took over organizing the international INOC-meetings.

Albrecht Schürhoff and Hildegard Werland who worked through the text from the perspective of a native speaker.

To the colleagues at isb, who have been engaged in this project, in particular to Lisa Meggendorfer, Almuth Pühra, Judith Schmid, Laura Sobez, Ingeborg Weidner, Heidi Wetzel and Bettina Gentner.

To all colleagues and customers who gave us the opportunity to learn and develop for almost 40 years.

Introduction

Culture comes from culture and examples teach the lesson.
(isb-slogan)

An organization is not a defined thing. An organization appears as something different depending on different chosen perspectives. The owner of a company may think of it in terms of legal construction and which shareholders hold which kind of share. The technical director may understand it as buildings and technical equipment, the HR director may understand it as a marketplace for qualification and performances, the training director may see an assembly of competences and needs for more qualification etc.

isb discusses organizations from a variety of perspectives, important for developing both professional and organizational culture, always related to people and performance. From a systemic perspective, a company may be seen as a network of leadership relationships, as a system of responsibilities or a system where learning takes place.

This illustrates that "systemic" is rather about a way of looking at things than about defining a company as a system, even though this can also be seen as a valid definition. It is based on the principle of taking ideas about reality as real even if they convey only a vague connection to factual reality. From a systemic perspective reality is always the reality of the observer. Isb observes companies from the perspective of relationships between human beings acting in their organizational roles. Culture of performance and satisfaction in working lives is our main perspective, because this is the core of our expertise. Our goal is to engage responsible executives and service providers who are ready to take a look at their work and their businesses from this perspective.

Our major focus on organizations is development through culture. Culture? Do we really have time and resources for cultural development? We should definitely invest it!

If you think culture is expensive, try ignorance!

Almost everybody has experienced that in a project after a quick start and achieving quick results, after some time problems start to pile up. Achieving good results becomes increasingly difficult and expensive, if you have neglected taking care of essential basics in the first place. If you go for quick wins by neglecting culture, this will backfire through problems in the longer run. However, if you take good care of culture from the beginning, your potential in gaining further results will grow steadily. The more complex the tasks of a team become and the faster conditions change, the more important the cultural foundation of the team tends to be.

If you want quick results,
start with culturing.

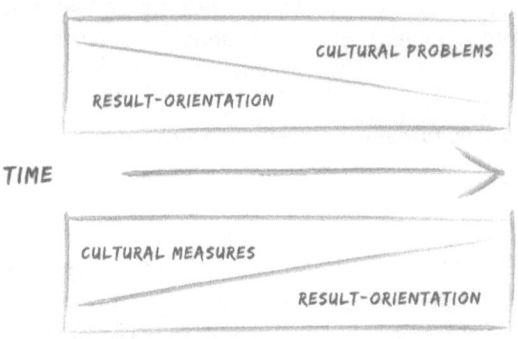

Fig. 1:   Relation of result and culture orientation in organizations
          (Schmid 1996)

There are no limits to the complexity in which an organization
can be looked at. We elaborate here on our perspectives and
approaches, as this is exactly our expertise. By doing that, we
feel responsible for serving the overall responsibility of entrepreneurship. This is crucial at the end of the day.

1. Sharing reality

Why sharing reality?

An organization is a mix of multiple realities functioning together to achieve results. These realities can either be cohesive or fragmented. If realities are not in sync, energy in an organization will be drained and there will be a waste of time, money, productivity and human energy. This is why sharing realities as a perspective matters for all areas in organizations. Looking at structures, processes, approaches, models and methods, there is always the one urgent question: is it contributing to a shared reality? Shared reality does not mean that everybody agrees on a certain point of view, nor do we want to reduce enriching variety. It simply means that we mutually understand as much of our realities as we possibly can. It means that we are able to effectively relate to each other and to join each other's realities in a way that makes organizational life and performance possible, effective and satisfying.

1.1. What is Reality?

From a systemic point of view, reality can only be grasped, if we understand whose reality is meant. Individuals and groups live in their own cosmos, with their own mix of habits of perceiving, varying experience in biography, interests, competences, responsibilities and roles in society. Although reality may include "hard facts", it is still a narrative. And many "hard facts" derive from ideas about reality having created their own reality in return. This is why in principle such realties should be open to change, provided that new ideas are created and realized in a shared process.

1.2. Creating reality by communication

A reality, which is not shared, can cause a lot of malfunctioning and dissatisfaction. Therefore, we must obviously be heading for better sharing wherever improving co-operation is intended. Simply stating individual reality as a valid and obligatory frame for everybody is usually not enough. It takes more to achieve active and creative co-operation. It requires communication on reality with those who have to be reached as co-creators of reality. This is exactly why a culture of communication and competence in dialogue on sharing reality is an art and a responsibility of its own importance. This goes far beyond simply improving one's ability of listening and self-expression. In the organizational field, we need models and approaches allowing specifications and combinations of sharing in many dimensions of role requirements and personal issues. The systemic communication approaches for the organizational field, which have been developed, practiced and taught at isb for decades exactly fit that challenge. They picture the isb cosmos of understanding professions and organizations as a systemic artwork of communication and culture.

1.3. Communication as cultural encounter

Let us start with a communication model focusing specifically on the encounter of different realities, serving us as an alternative to the traditional Shannon Weaver "sender-channel-receiver model" of communication (Fig. 2).

Fig. 2:   traditional sender-channel-receiver communication model

The sender-channel-receiver model represents the traditional technical idea of a "controlled" perspective on communication. It is to be expected that the reality of sender A when sent through the communication channel turns identically to the reality of receiver B. If transferred, it suggests that also human communication functions in a controllable way. If the receiver's reality doesn't respond in the expected way, someone has a problem. From this perspective, those creative aspects arising out of the communicators' cultural background that change the effect intended are not accepted. The communication partners are expected to keep such creative extensions as misfunction out of communication.

By contrast, the cultural encounter model of communication (Fig. 3) assumes that each communication partner has their own reality and uses the encounter to promote personal realities and developments. This model considers it as normal that these realities differ, and need to be connected if something like a shared reality is supposed to ensue. The creation of shared reality requires a necessary effort in communication and a specific competence. The cultural encounter model of communication gives up the idea of controlled communication, as the realities of living organisms are complex leaving them unable to even control it themselves. Everybody has to acknowledge that there will be surprises. Starting from this perspective alters both the way we deal with unexpected results of communication and how we go about connecting with each other.

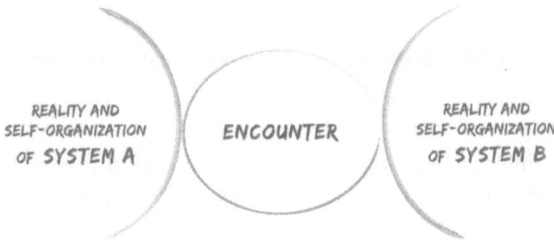

Fig. 3:   Cultural encounter model of communication (Schmid 1991)

1.4.   Four levels of shared reality

Here a brief introduction of the systemic term "information" as it is an important basis for the following cultural encounter model of communication.

Information:

From a systemic perspective, data and information are two different things. Data refers to facts of any kind. However, only those facts that make a difference to someone result in information. Look at this example: "It is raining" is a statement.

Let us put this into the context of hiking. If we do not go hiking on a rainy day, the difference between "raining" and "not raining" becomes relevant information with regard to hiking. If we do go hiking on a rainy day as well, "raining" has no information value for the decision of whether we go hiking or not, but it might have for the question of whether to "bring an umbrella" or "not bring an umbrella".

Thus, for communication to be successful, a shared frame of reference, i.e. a shared framework for the confrontation of realities needs to be established. For this purpose, we distinguish between four levels of a shared reality.

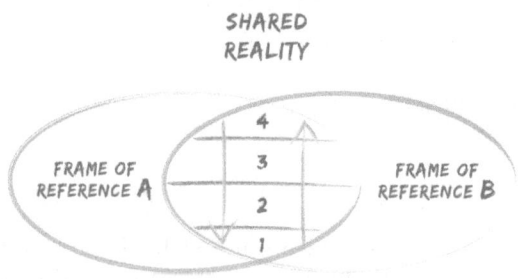

Level 4: Shared understanding of responsibilities and achievements
Level 3: Shared understanding of how people and things interact
Level 2: Shared meaning and relevance of perspectives and facts
Level 1: Shared perspectives and facts to be taken into account

Fig. 4: 4 Levels in creating a shared reality (Schmid/Hipp 1998)

Let us continue the example above. Although hiking was previously agreed, B doesn't show up. When confronted, B replies: "I was assuming we could not possibly go hiking together while it is raining!"

Level 1: Perspectives and Data

Are A and B referring to the same data? Do they both know the factual situation to which the other is referring by the sentence "It is raining"? Or would B say so when it is cloudy, whereas A would only do so if it's raining cats and dogs? Let's assume both would agree on using the sentence whenever there is some rain.

Level 2: Meanings and relevance

Do participants attribute the same meanings to existing data? Do A and B share the same dimensions and directions of relevance? Or do they draw different conclusions? "Rain can lead to sickness and not acceptable risks for individual and the enterprise" vs. "Rain doesn't create risks, only acceptable individual discomfort".

Level 3: Interdependencies and interaction

What conclusions can be derived from the frame of reference and the interrelations between different elements? Do A and B share imaginations of the means by which the desired realities can be created or changed? Or do they differ like "coping with rain is a question of equipment" vs. "...a question of personal fitness"?

Level 4: Responsibilities and achievements

"The group leader is in charge of precautions for possible dangers, checking everybody's fitness and providing equipment. If he considers these not sufficient, he has to refuse participation."

In many cases where fairly reliable agreements on the level of achievements and responsibilities are reached, shared reality on the other levels is easily assumed. But hidden disagreements on levels 1-3 can lead to non-complementary actions at any time. If shared reality is to be ensured and hidden dissent is detected, all levels of reality encounter need to be checked. Conflicts often escalate on level 4, simply because the checking of all other levels of constructing reality has been neglected. A step-by-step clarification may help to improve mutual understanding to de-escalate conflicts.

Do participants share ideas of what might be acceptable solutions to open questions? Do A and B share ideas about their responsibility for these solutions? "Everybody is responsible for their own fitness as well as bringing equipment and for bearing the consequences in case of getting in trouble" vs.

Confrontation

We mostly associate the term 'confrontation' with conflict and quarrel. However, from a more neutral perspective, the term simply refers to the encounter of different realities. Confrontation, based on mutual respect, can be of great advantage for the systems involved, enabling them to constructively deal with differences, and thus contributing to sharing realities and community building. But even "positive" attempts frequently fail, especially if the respective communicative task is underestimated and if the culture of positive confrontation is underdeveloped. The purpose of confrontation is not necessarily to achieve the same realities, but rather to strengthen the self-reflection, the dynamics and identity of the systems involved: "The encounter with the otherness can strengthen your uniqueness." (Rupert Lay).

Cultural encounters can certainly be satisfying without this model. Wherever this is not the case, it might be helpful to reflect on the process of sharing reality described above. If some difficult situations are resolved in a positive confrontation climate, there are generally positive effects on other areas. As people involved learn a lot in the process, they can help spreading this kind of awareness and clarifying communication for others.

1.5. Communication as dialogue

Reality shared by human beings involves a lot more than usually intended. This multitude of influences is not only a source of misunderstandings; it also contributes to creative and meaningful reality. To be able to benefit from that richness, it is helpful to define communication as "dialogue". Dialogue means "through the word" or more generally "through the surface". In communication below surfaces many more aspects of reality are connected than we are aware of.

The following dialogue model of communication (Fig. 5) focuses on partners understanding and mutually influencing each other on both a conscious and an unconscious level. It is based on the assumption that partners first 'psyche out' each other intuitively. Then they decide on how to continue further dealings with each other.

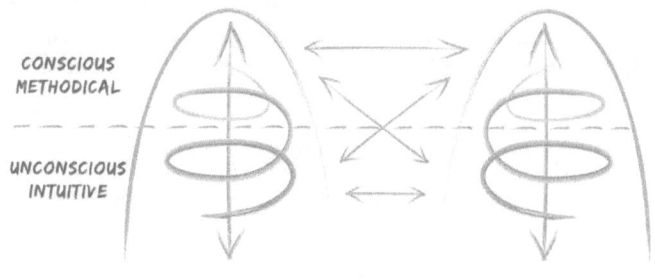

Fig. 5:   Dialogue model of communication (Schmid 1998)

By conscious methodical surface we understand the part of communication we can control. Meaningful and creative co-operation only takes place whenever this surface is created in accordance with and serving the reality behind it. The conscious methodical mode has the function of controlling in the sense of setting frameworks for the communication process. But sharing reality in a deeper sense depends on encounters on many surfaces and backgrounds. These more complex aspects of reality have to be recognized, respected and shaped. For this purpose, a communication culture should be provided which is sensitive and is able to deal with whatever appears from unconscious intuitive spheres. Meaning is mostly created on intuitive levels and shows up as feelings (felt sense). This is why educated intuitive judgments are particularly important in professional relationships. After all, both the methodical and the intuitive level inspire and control each other.

1.6. Supporting Dialogue Culture

Complex processes cannot just be controlled from the surface, as this would leave essential parts in the unknown. Therefore, the conscious part of a controlling person needs to adopt the attitude of an ethnologist. Conversation should become a stage, on which the forces of the unconscious levels can be lived, observed and shaped. This is why a meta goal of all developmental communication should be the improvement of dialogue communication culture.

How can we understand and shape the surface of communication so that meanings and energy from background levels are positively included? How can we acquire methods, which address and connect intuitive levels of perception and communication? Conscious methods should be sensitive, creating new surface forms in order to remain connected with background levels whilst acting as a facilitator or supervisor rather than as a controller.

2. Sharing systems of roles

All the world's a stage, and all the men and women merely players ... and one man in his time plays many parts – Shakespeare

2.1. Why roles?

Everyone has experienced that humans can be different in different moments. As a professional colleague someone may argue confidently and clearly, as a subordinate, he may act as a hypocrite or a rebel, and as a companion during a private meeting, he may be empathetic and charming. Obviously, he organizes himself and his relationships in different ways, according to actual dominant realities. This role concept can take into account such observations.

The roles we play in life are crucial to shaping our personality, our life course and careers. Professional communication in organizations can be lived in a much more qualified way if the corresponding roles are activated and performed appropriately. Roles as a focus can help us to look at people and their communication, especially to develop role competencies and to organize role relationships. In this role concept, relationships in context and content are considered role-to-role. This role concept is special, because it integrates dimensions beyond psychological aspects.

2.2. Roles connect individuals and organization

The way in which people and organizations are approached in their encounter is inevitably a matter of choice. The models that we choose for the description define the characteristics and types of relationships to be dealt with. Many approaches differentiate between personality and organization and provide only vague descriptions of how they relate to each other. In contrast, we assign roles to individuals in an organization as well as to the structure of organizations discussing both aspects with one language. Fig. 6

In encounters of individuals and organizations it is not possible to refer to the totality of both. The questions are: How much individual? How much organization?

Fig. 6:   Organizational Roles:
          the encounter individual – organization (Schmid 2017)

Organizational roles work wherever they are positively aligned with backgrounds of individuals and their organization. Discussing roles and balancing the individual and organization connects individual and organizational development.

2.3.   What are roles?

Like many components of the theater metaphor, "role" is ex-perienced as well-known and is easy to understand without being defined. Nevertheless, let us look at a formal definition:

A role is a coherent system of attitudes, feelings, behavior, perspective on reality and the accompanying relationships in which they operate.

In this definition, each role is linked to a particular sphere of reality and related frames of reference, and includes the rela-tionships in which these roles are played. Most of the time roles are lived out without much reflection and thus ideas about the kind of relationships roles shape and suggest are invited.

Illustration:

Both the variety and the importance of roles are immediately comprehensible when you consider the following example: Imagine a traffic accident with people involved, their neigh-bors, the technical aid operations officer, the ambulance, the police responsible for securing the scene of the accident and any future evidence, and a colleague passing by incidentally. We can imagine many other roles that - depending on the event - activate the role players' own attitudes, feelings and behaviors and their own perspectives on reality. All of them are concerned with certain aspects of reality and offer ideas on how to shape relationships with other people present at the scene of the accident. If the firefighter chief of operations happens to be a personal friend of one of the critically injured and maybe godfather of the person's son who is present but unhurt, we can imagine that multiple roles are activated simul-taneously and that they co-existent within this one person having to be balanced in such a situation.

2.4.　Roles and three worlds

In the isb -role-model personality is described as the portfolio of his/her roles being played on the stages of his/her world.

Described as a "three-world model", personality is defined as sets of roles that operate in three worlds, the private world, the organizational world and the professional world. Each one faces a variety of challenges, depending on whether an organizational role (e.g. a women's rights department representative), a professional role (e.g. social worker) or a private role (e.g. mother) is of primary importance.

Figure 7 shows the personality composed of roles in these three worlds, distinguishing the role repertoire in organizational, professional and private roles. The role areas can be used to analyze role communication as shown below.

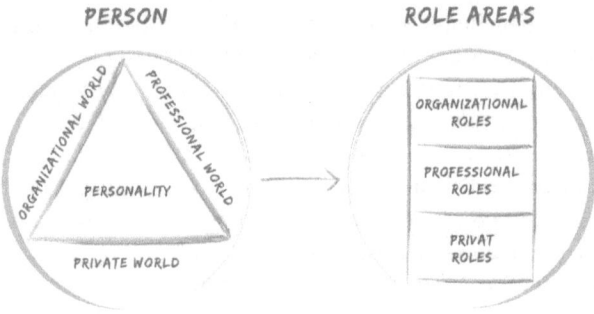

Fig. 7:　Three-world personality model and role-ladder model (Schmid 1994)

Discussion:

Does the role model reduce people to "playing roles" instead of being complete human personalities? Definitely not. In this model, there is no difference between humans and their roles, because personality is defined as a composite of roles. For pragmatic reasons, the model implies that humanity of people is expressed and experienced through their roles, as in the theater metaphor life was considered to be a series of scenes. The uniqueness and humanity are expressed through one's way of playing role in life. Thus, people are uniquely associated with plays and stages of their worlds through living roles that are co-determined by them and others. Personality and communication are thus seen also as a matter of context and content that relates to society.

2.5.   Discussing personality

As we use the role model discussing personality, it fits in with many considerations and approaches of Transactional Analysis (TA).

Here are some examples:

Under the headline role integration and resource policy questions about the autonomy and functioning of an adult can be discussed. Nowadays, professionals are required in an ever-increasing variety of roles and have to combine different affiliations to different systems and their frame of reference. Therefore, it is unlikely that you identify with a role or with a small, manageable bundle of roles. Rather, an autonomous, professional attitude has to be acquired in the selection and shape of roles, as well as in the decision on and control of affiliations. Putting together the network of roles and references in their own way is a challenge in itself.

However, we are also confronted with conflicts between different affiliations and roles. It proves essential to manage the available resources economically, including one's own energy and time resources. In the modern business world, many professionals are generally overwhelmed by the large role demands placed on them, unless they manage to control complexity by means of their own autonomous identity and congruently bundle the role configurations into viable structures.

In addition to individual role ideas, there are expectations and a judgment on how a role is played. Roles can only be played competently in interaction with others and in understanding them playing their roles.

Role Competence means to control the coherent system of attitudes, feelings, behavior, perspective on reality, and the accompanying relationships bundled in the role. This includes understanding and matching the intended play. Many personality problems stem from the fact that the need to acquire role-playing skills is either not recognized or not taken seriously, with insufficient steps being taken to acquire them.

Headlines such as the **activation of roles**, **leading roles** and the **executive power** stand for further consideration.

Professionalism has much to do with the ability to intentionally activate and deactivate certain roles and also to provide triggers for other stakeholders. This has a lot to do with structuring situations, but also with controlling one's own internal functioning on the one hand and on the other the ability to address roles in others through communication. It is equally important to be able to decide on and follow one's own roles. Thus, the ability of managing role systems is touched. Which is the role that controls the process to integrate more roles and switch back and forth? Do the leading roles have the executive power to orchestrate other roles?

Restrictions of personality are discussed as role management limitations, such as role fixation, role exclusion, role contamination, role confusion, rigid role habits and conventions. These terms are somehow self-explanatory and have been discussed elsewhere. Many considerations from the concept of Ego states are easy to apply and expand.

By way of illustration, I refer to role contamination as a chronic inclusion of disturbing elements of other roles in a role currently played, without the person being aware of it. While the person may consider the included elements as appropriate, partners are irritated. For example, collective bargaining in a negotiating partner role can lead to outrage if the individual is worried about the expected wage reduction for him as an individual. These feelings are easily confused with appropriate feelings of the negotiating role. In another example, someone may activate behaviors in a private relationship as he would do as a psychotherapist, without identifying them as alien to private role relationship. This phenomenon is known as professional deformation.

2.6.   Discussing communication and relationships

The isb-role-model can be used to describe communication. The diagram of the ladder model is used to illustrate interaction. In Figure 8, only three role areas are distinguished. If more or different role areas and roles are needed, further differentiations can be made.

31

The communication units represented by arrows are called transactions. When using such a diagram, it needs to be clarified which role initiates the transaction, what role it is targeted to, and which role provides the answer.

There are transactions considered as open in the foreground (solid line arrows) and transactions considered as hidden in the background (dotted arrows). Thus, messages on the front stage are differentiated from those on the backstage. The numbers in Fig. 8 relate to the example below.

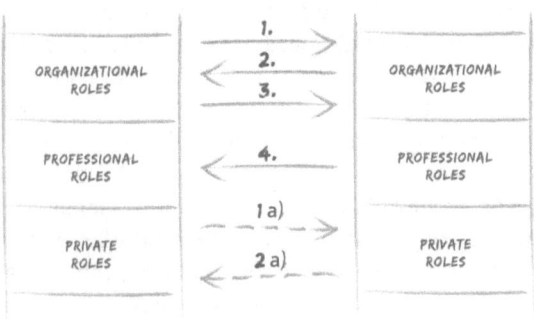

Fig. 8: Analyzing communication using the role model (Schmid 1994)

Let us look at this example:

Imagine a strategy discussion between the head of HR-department and his team, with the agenda "setting priorities".

Initially, discussion takes place at the level of organizational roles where people can make suggestions according to the corporate culture, but the final decision is left to the head of HR (transaction 1./2.). After some time, unnoticed by the participants, there is a switch to professional arguments (transaction 3./4.) in which some people feel dominated by hierarchy. In the background, there could also irritate a male rivalry around a woman. The psychological approach may suggest directing attention to this background and thus solving the irritation. The organizational approach may direct attention to the role change and role relationships. Restoring stable communication between organizational roles, in which hierarchy has to set priorities, may solve the problem. The psychological perspective, the focus on the private background only refers to one kind of background analysis.

Here is an example for an organizational background: Two members of a department – such as the communication trainer and training administrator – tend to have the same conflicts over and over. They may think they have problems working together as professionals and try to treat the problem as differences in their professional approaches. However, they can overlook the fact that the difficulties in their relationship are caused even more by the background of the organizational structure with, for example, incompatible, doubly defined areas of responsibility and incompatible goals.

Organizational roles can influence relationship issues from the background. In this case, the dotted arrows represent this influence as hidden transactions due to role backgrounds in that particular organization.

To clarify such situations, it is important to emphasize the background relationship between the organizational roles, in order to bring them to the foreground making it the primary focus of attention. Otherwise, escalations may lead to various neurotic reactions requiring unnecessary psychotherapeutic work. When resolved at the organizational level, people can consciously return to competent behavior and good relationships as the organization has become more functional and healthier.

3. Sharing responsibility

3.1. What is responsibility?

Organizations can be characterized as being responsible for performance and development. This can only be achieved, if a number of players act responsibly, both individually and in interplay with others. An organization can even be described as a system of responsibilities (see more in Chapt. 5.1 What is an organization?). Clarifying both individual and collective responsibilities as well as dialoguing on these responsibilities is key to specifying encounters and communication in organizations. This is why we have described the culture of an organization in terms of responsibility.

"Responsible" is derived from "respond-able", "responsibility" basically means "being able to respond". This may describe the ability of an individual, a team or an organization as a whole. Obligation is only part of this. Usually support from others and resources are also required. Furthermore, responsibility will not work without motivation and competence of individuals and systems. The model given below (Fig. 9) can help identify the intervention point by which shared responsibility in organization can be facilitated.

3.2. Four Dimensions of responsibility

Fig. 9: Four dimensions of a responsibility system
(Schmid/Messmer 2004)

Four dimensions of responsibility go together: Values, Qualification, Resources and Accountability:

People should be willing to give required responses, because it fits their values and intentions. (Values)

People should be able to give responses, because it fits their qualifications. (Qualification)

The organization should provide necessary resources like entitlement, equipment, money etc. (Resources)

The organization should oblige people to give responses and provide consequences, if not given (Accountability).

Especially highly committed people often try to give responses without sufficient conditions being met. This is due to confusion of the dimensions or of who has to contribute what to the overall responsibility. Whether responsibility can generally be increased and in a balanced way depends on identifying lacking ingredients. Here are two examples: when an adequate response fails, employees sometimes go for more training, because they believe this is due to a lack of qualification. They may not be aware that, if the equipment was adequate, their qualification would be sufficient. Thus, they tend to compensate inadequate equipment by additional qualification. Or: Expected responses fail, even though both resources and qualification are adequate. But what people are really lacking is motivation, as for instance the expected response does not fit their values.

3.3. Responsible for the whole?

Responsibility is not restricted to what an individual can be hold accountable for. Responsibility shall be understood and designed as complementary, referring to related parts of the whole system. In some way, every member of an organization is also responsible for the whole system of responsibilities. Thus, defining responsibility matching what an individual is directly responsible for, is not enough.

We therefore distinguish between (see Fig. 10):

1. Responsibility for… a certain job with corresponding tasks and performance. This responsibility implicitly includes formal obligation which, if neglected, can have legal consequences.
2. Responsibility related to…a particular cooperation with others e.g. (internal and external) "customers" and "suppliers" in value gaining and leadership processes. "Responsibility related to" also requires the development and

maintenance of organizational ethics as well as one's own commitment in integrating individual actions into the system as a whole.

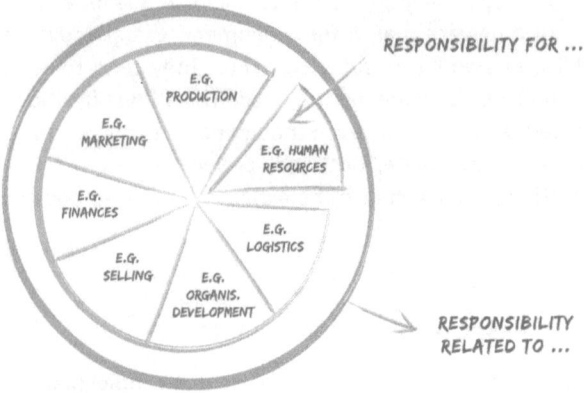

Fig. 10:   The system of complementary and related responsibility
(Schmid/Messmer 2004)

3.4.   Dialoguing on Responsibility

By definition, the logic of shared responsibility in organizations is not a "natural" but an explicitly or implicitly created reality. Due to changes in the organization, the responsibility system usually has to be revised and further developed from time to time, especially if new questions require new answers. Even while the responsibility system is still functional, members of the organization may be engaged in an active open dialogue, striving to keep the culture alive for everybody, especially for newly recruited team members. In many areas adaptations of this kind are part of daily business.

Questions useful in responsibility dialogues:

1. Which answers to known and still valid questions are no longer satisfying?

2. Are there new questions requiring new answers?

3. Who is expected to give what kind of answers?

4. Are all four dimensions of responsibility available to everybody?

5. Are dimensions of responsibility missing or consistently weak?

6. Are other dimensions being overstressed in order to compensate this?

3.5. Avoiding responsibility

If clarifying responsibilities through dialogue leads to satisfying solutions no further effort is needed. But often operating attitudes and behaviors can be characterized as avoiding responsibility. Here we find that responsibility cannot be adequately established and vanishes or is shifted to those who are unable to take over or have to make inadequate efforts. Missing responsibility causes discomfort. This discomfort is often shifted to those who do not own the responsibility. Discomfort may indicate that responsibility is avoided.

If someone tries to start a dialogue on responsibility, there are often avoiding, blocking or misleading reactions instead of supporting the interest to clarify responsibility. This may have different reasons, which could be interesting to find out.

But communication about reasons is rarely possible and trying to talk about them might tighten things unnecessarily. More importantly, those experiencing discomfort should identify its causes and how they can be transformed into requests for responsible behavior.

It is important to actively and specifically invite others into responsibility. While this inviting can be done usually only through communication, a variety of mistakes can be made. Emotionally involved people may use inappropriate communication channels, inviting reactions to their style rather than to their request. However, even excellent inviters may not be successful - especially if the other side has more power. Without own power, people only have an impact on the other side if the invitation is voluntarily accepted. Those who have the power to ignore the invitation without consequences may choose to misuse their power.

Often even experienced professionals do not know how to attribute discomfort to avoiding or shifting responsibility. Or they do not know how to adequately confront others about missing responsibility. Being explicitly confronted with competent invitations to responsibility makes avoidance less easy. Transactional Analysis offers criteria to diagnose dysfunctional symbiotic relationships.

Criteria for dysfunctional symbiotic relationships:

1. responsibility is not taken, or

2. responsibility is shifted, or

3. discomfort about missing responsibility is shifted, or

4. confrontations on discomfort or responsibility are blocked or misled, and thus

5. options and potentials for improving responsibility are either not used or not developed.

3.6. Inviting Responsibility

At the isb, inviting responsibility is part of professional training.

Often, we start by creating awareness of discomfort. Shared discomfort may be the first step to responsibility dialogue. To go beyond just complaining, we suggest starting an analysis by asking questions such as:

Diagnose-Fragen zu Verantwortung:

1. Am I experiencing discomfort?

2. Is my discomfort possibly related to missing responsibility?

3. Who do I feel matters in this context?

4. What are the relevant questions?

5. Who should give answers?

6. Can the four dimensions of responsibility (see above) help differentiate?

7. Is there someone who avoids accepting questions and giving answers?

8. How and by which mechanism is shifting of responsibility and/or discomfort taking place?

9. What are possible reasons for this? Who can exert influence?

10. What would have to be changed to improve both clarifying and taking care of responsibility?

11. Whose discomfort will then be diminished? Would this create new discomfort or new questions of responsibility at other points in the organization?

12. How should shared learning on the responsibility system be further developed?

At the isb, analyzing avoidance and responsibility step-by-step is part or the training. Beyond that, ways in which confrontation and invitation can be powerfully communicated are trained as well. However, with people either in power or not reachable through convincing communication, thus insisting on avoiding responsibility, the problem cannot be solved by communication alone.

4.   Sharing Leadership

Leadership plays a vital role in running and developing an organization. Leadership can promote effectiveness and orientation, making leadership one of the oldest principles of organizing processes in evolution. While still holding this importance, leadership needs to be redefined toward our current reality in several ways. Recent approaches emphasize emerging organizational processes or even replacing hierarchy totally. However, for most people responsible for running an effective organization it is obvious that hierarchical leadership should not be replaced, but be combined with self-organization of people and emerging processes. Freedom, creativity and self-organizing is precious, but needs to be framed within a context and towards the purpose of an organization as well as the organizational culture the organization stands for. Such framing and building-up of an appropriate culture is the essential task of leadership. However, looking at leadership as individual behavior is not sufficient. A leadership culture where many players can be active in sharing leadership for the overall health of the organization is needed. In this chapter we will focus various aspects of leadership from a systemic perspective.

4.1.   What is leadership?

Leadership is a matter of relationships. Leading people means successfully inviting them into performing within a given frame or into helping to create a new one. This is the isb-definition of leadership. If you analyze or train leadership, the smallest unit should be the leadership relationship, as leading is the interaction between everybody involved. After all, leadership competence is needed from all partners being part of the leadership relationship. Leading can only be as good as the leadership relationship allows. The leader needs to understand that there is a mutual dependency and in so far have a humble attitude towards all partners in that relationship.

To illustrate this, here is the story of a first lesson in horse jumping.

I was already a quite good rider and in good co-ordination with my horse "Abruzze". One day my riding teacher put a one-foot high obstacle in the middle the riding court and told me to jump with Abruzze over it. What I didn't know is that jumping is not a natural behavior of a horse and Abruzze was no more trained on jumping than I was. My teacher (a former military cavalier) instructed me to gallop towards the obstacle and to bend a bit forward in order to make it easier for Abruzze to jump. Just before the obstacle Abruzze stemmed her legs into the sand and bent her head down. The only one, who overcame the obstacle was flying me, landing uncomfortably in the mud. The next time I bent backwards thus managing to stay on Abruzze when Abruzze stopped again. But then she jumped. And being totally inexperienced she made a huge jump cata-pulting me into the mud again, an experience I repeated al-most a dozen times during this lesson.

Having watched my training, an experienced rider offered me to do some jumping with his horse well-trained in jumping. And I learned very fast with that horse. I just had to go with the horse's competence. Of course, my competence dropped im-mediately when being back on Abruzze. It was yet a different challenge introducing an untrained horse through the process of jumping.

4.2. Leadership communication

Leadership communication does not just mean transferring messages as to how things should be seen or done. Leadership means interaction and co-operation. In order to achieve this, the specificity of functioning and communication in leadership encounters has to be understood.

As tasks, people and circumstances differ, there is no such thing as right leadership. There is only functioning leadership and there are many styles in which leadership can function. Which style works depends on the context and matching between the people involved. Leadership is self-sustaining, whenever all involved organize themselves with positive respect to the intent and style of leadership. This is why it is of very limited value to define leadership behavior as personal attribute and to run training programs merely "teaching" how to be a leader. Instead, leadership relationships and styles of interplay within these encounters should be in the focus. The communication models described before may serve as a basis. (see Chapt. 1.3/1.5)

4.3. Leadership network

Taylorism allows managing complex processes effectively through fragmentation and role differentiation. But it also results in the fact that nobody can achieve results of complex processes on their own. Instead, everybody depends on the other. Performance and culture can only be accomplished together. This is also true for leadership, especially strategic leadership. Impulses for strategic developments have to go through various chains of leadership relationships in order to be realized in an organization. Hierarchical leadership is increasingly seen as only one contribution to a wider and more complex leadership system.

Every chain is as strong as its weakest part. In order to make strategic enterprises work, attention should be directed to all parts of the leadership chain preferably strengthening the weakest parts. The more leadership relationships and their styles differ in various areas of an organization, the higher the challenge to keep them working together. The less well a business area is functioning, the stronger the need of attention in leadership development, even though this might not appear as rewarding at first glance. This is what defines leadership responsibility in relation to the whole chain or the whole network.

4.4. Leadership versus Management

Leadership, as usually understood, includes two dimensions of creating reality. One is designing structures and processes, the other is communicating and relating to people involved. We define the designing function as management and the communication function as leadership.

The theater metaphor (further described in Chapt. 10.9) can help clarifying this distinction. If in theater you have to create a new play, you usually need a script of the intended play. Based on the idea about what to put into action, - the so-called plot -, somebody has to design a storyline putting the basic story into sequences of action. The script defines the events and the way to tell the story, as well as by whom and how everything should be enacted. Above all, the scriptwriter needs imagination and designing competence.

Furthermore, you need a director, i.e. somebody involving and instructing actors step-by-step, so they understand both their roles and how to interact telling the story in the intended way. A director of a play needs communication competence, a feeling for actors and a vision about how they can interact.

Usually leaders are either more talented as designers or as communicators.

If both, designing competence and communication competence, are not available within the same person, then the two functions have to co-operate in different ways. This results in a variety of approaches and styles in creating new plays. Some focus more on the magic of a good script, others on the magic of good relationship and communication while enacting. If this is not clarified and the presence and integration of both talents and forces is just assumed, difficult processes of dealing with deficits and ways of compensating may occur.

If the main leader is predominantly a designer, he needs communicators at his side, helping to transform the script into the shared reality of the players. If the main leader is more focused on relationships and communication, he needs designer qualities as a complement making sure that the play actually tells the intended story. There do not have to be two official roles like scriptwriter and director, respectively manager and leader present, but the ingredients and qualities required should be available.

4.5.   Operational versus strategic leadership

There is another important difference in the area of leadership, i.e. operational versus strategic leadership. Operational leadership maintains known processes and their qualities, probably with changing players. Strategic leadership is heading for further developing known processes or creating new ones.

Referring to the theater metaphor, strategic leadership is needed if a new play has to be orchestrated or an existing play is to be re-enacted in a renewed fashion. As described in the chapter above, the director of a newly enacted play has to be much more creative in terms of designing the new play and staffing it with actors who are not used to playing it. Once a new play has been established and performed several times, the role of directing further replays changes. Now a day-by-day director can do the work, merely responsible for keeping up the level of performance. Competences in designing anew are now less important, whereas maintaining care for reproduction and the company become more vital. In the end both ways of directing are important for theaters playing their shows over a long time but still different in many ways. Certainly, both of these qualities and passions should not be separated. After all, a new play should be designed in such a way that it can be easily replayed in good quality, with changing staff and in different surrounding. Without ensuring perpetual renewal and changes plays cannot be kept attractive and alive.

Companies starting their business with new products, processes and positioning in the market first need plenty of strategic leadership. But in order to succeed with repetition of high-quality processes, they also need a lot of operational leadership, especially for introducing and involving new staff. Both qualities of leadership have to respect each other, working hand in hand. If strategic leadership habitually dominates operational leadership, a company may be unnecessarily stirred up in their routines of everyday performance. Vice versa, operational leaders may block necessary strategic developments, sticking too much to their routines. In strategic leadership one has to provide the system with explanations much more comprehensively and frequently than ever expected, especially in the starting phase of new strategies or new cultural developments. Talented strategic leaders tend to underestimate the necessity to invest in sharing and stabilizing ideas with others. If a company culture ensures a lot of shared leadership in both dimensions, both daily performance and necessary change and development benefit sustainably.

4.6. Power and authority in leadership

Leading means successfully inviting others into performing within an existing play or helping to create a new one. What does this have to do with power and authority?

For a command-and-obey relationship, "inviting" seems to be quite a romantic exaggeration. But making others perform in a complex reality cannot be done without their self-directed behavior. Establishing leadership involves offering and using power on the one hand and accepting or co-creating power on the other hand. Thus, both empowerment and attributing authority constitute this dimension of a leadership relationship.

From the leader's perspective, something needs to be offered that convinces others to organize themselves in a co-operative way. To achieve this, the leader contributes ideas, and so do those who are being led. If they fail to empower the leader, his power is not real. Leadership only takes effect, if power and empowerment match. Power and empowerment are twins.

Authority is achieved either as granted by authority structures or by mutual agreement. This can be explicit (by contract) or implicit (by complementary behavior).

The isb differentiates between three dimensions and sources of power: power of sovereignty, power of sense-making and power of the creator. (cf. Fig. 11)

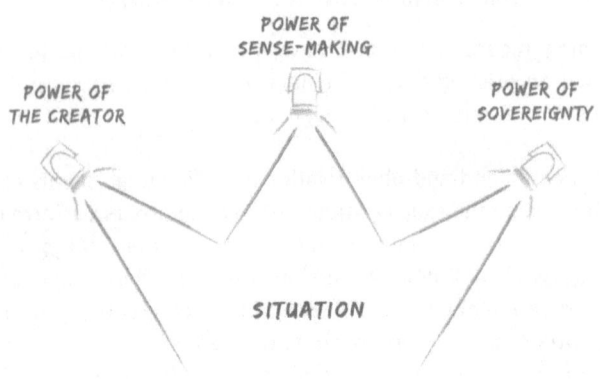

Fig. 11: Dimensions of power and perspectives
(Schmid/Messmer, 2003)

Power of sovereignty is usually authorized through the power structure of an organization. It is assigned to the organizational role of the leaders and gives them the right to define the reality to be seen as valid and the behavior to be seen as obligatory. This generates the empowerment through adapting fitting this kind of power. Those who are led are obliged to accept the power through their contract with the organization related to their organizational roles. They can only avoid this through denial or by leaving the role and this relationship.

Power of sense-making is based on the leader being perceived as someone who represents meaningful values, ideas and purposes. Strong power of this kind is defined as charisma. Others feel moved and become followers, ready to organize themselves oriented towards these forces. This generates the empowerment through following fitting this kind of power.

This power can be trained only to a limited extent as it is mostly based on attitudes and forces which people simply perceive or assume behind organizational roles.

Power of the creator is based on the belief that someone is capable of playing a leading role in creating realities. Others experience or believe that orienting themselves alongside these talents and contributing to these creations is more useful than doing something else. This constitutes the empowerment through expecting success fitting this kind of power. Although there should be some talent available, know-how and competence as a creator can be gained through education.

The presence and impact of these three dimensions of power is to be seen as complementary and as a matter of combinations. Can each person reflect which power is used and gained? What is his or her specific style? What kind of empowerment is one heading for? What kind of power are they ready to accept or invite? And which are one's preferences in giving or withholding authority?

There may well be other sources and dimensions of power. In the isb approach, power is a matter of co-creation and relationship, as leading is a matter of co-operation and sharing reality.

4.7.   Leadership styles

There is no such thing as "right leadership" - there is only functioning leadership. Whatever the right choice may be can only be judged in the light of both the people involved and the situation. Therefore, appropriate leadership constructions and styles may differ for different purposes, in different fields and relationships. This can be illustrated by two different leadership cultures around two dance company directors in Germany, both charismatic and internationally successful. The one led primarily by creating a space for careful awareness for one's own ideas and developments, while only from time to time mirroring her perceptions of dancers and contributions. Script and directing for each piece of dance was to unfold during practice, following the impulses from the dancers. In contrast, the other starts from elaborated designs. He illustrates his ideas by modeling through dancing himself and arranging his dancers' body-to-body. It is likely that in both cases those directors and dancers have found each other because styles matched, each different but very successful in their own way. If both were to create a shared dance performance show, they should not decide in favor of one or the other style and leadership culture, but rather find ways to perform together accepting and valuing the differences.

We may choose to look at leadership subcultures in organizations in a similar way. In order to make them compatible for working together, a basis of awareness and dialogue between the protagonists is needed.

4.8.   Improving leadership relationships

As a basis for leadership development, leadership relationships are essential. The smallest unit is composed of two people bound together in a leadership relationship together wanting to improve their specific relationship. Both need to be basically competent in playing their roles and finding out how they can match. Also, they need to understand how their individual characters, the definitions of their roles and tasks, and how their context influences their relationship i.e. the way they individually relate to each other. They may find ways to improve their relationship or find out that somehow, they do not sufficiently match in order to prove investment into this relationship reasonable. In the frame of more complex leadership learning processes, this perspective of leadership relationship could be extended to leadership chains and networks in daily work or even used for upcoming OD-projects. Dealing with questions of leadership is also part of systems learning described in Chapt. 7.7.

4.9.   Leadership development

Members of leadership relationships should come together for training and supervision, in order to further develop their own interaction. This is a challenge for HR, as organizations and education approaches of leadership differ. Basically, everybody is challenged to integrate different styles in varying relationships. Besides, personal style preferences as well as the logic of roles, tasks, knowhow, power etc. should be taken in account. As no leadership trainer can possibly know about all these specifics, possibilities of a pre-defined training are very limited. Rather arranging dialogues between those who are in real leadership relationships should be at the center of leadership education.

As a basis, all people involved in a leadership development should share the same understanding of the intended leadership culture with all its shared features and varieties.

5. Sharing understanding on team and organization

5.1. What is an Organization?

An organization is a "projection" our of multiple perspectives. An chief executive of the organization may look at it from the angle of market share, the finance director may look at it from the view of economics, stakeholders may view it from the point of scalability, distribution partners may perceive it as business opportunity, employees may view it from the perspective of career growth. In each case the term organization resonates differently: it is the specific perspective on organization that makes the difference. Even though facts may be the same, choices of attributes and descriptions under the label "organization" are different. As a lot of different people work for an organization, each of them may look at it from their own unique perspective. When asked to name events representing organization, different people will select different events to be in the foreground. When discussing organizations, it is useful to differentiate between the perspectives involved and the question to which events they actually refer.

Fig. 12:   Perspectives on Organizations Model (Schmid 2016)

5.2.   Team – a question of specification

Whenever the term "team" appears, we feel intrigued to know what is actually meant. Team workshops are a type of service to easily be acquired, simply because of this illusion. If we take a closer look, we will detect either an unclear or a quite schematic understanding of what "the team" might be. Sometimes all people working on the same floor or in the same function are called a team, sometimes all those people who somehow should become involved are considered part of the team. Consequently, many team sessions or team workshops are confusing or ineffective. They rather appear to be some kind of group events, raising considerable group dynamics due to both the lack of clear focus and the hunger for attention of people present. In all those situations, people seem to be unclear about their part in the play.

However, if the purpose of a team meeting is unclear, it is difficult to select those who should be involved. In many cases decisions are made without important owners of related responsibilities. In other cases, so many players are invited creating a large group event clearly exceeding "team size". This tends to create unnecessary stress, complexity and costs.

5.3. Team – those who share responsibility

Thus the isb defines "team" as "those who share responsibility" or a community sharing responsibility. This means that clarification is required, in which context and for which purpose a group of people is called "team" with reference to a specific event. Imagine a situation of problems accepting a new IT-tool-supported process. You can look at the problems as generated through the tool and problems with handling and in matching other tools and processes. Then the key players and specialists for these kinds of questions should meet, e.g. a selection of users, (high and low performing), the developers of the tool and their principals, leaders responsible for the integration process, etc. They constitute the team at this moment.

Or you can look at the same situation as a resistance phenomenon evolving from habitual behavior leading to realistic fears as losing jobs through new tools and irrational anxieties. Then you would want to involve other players, as well such as employees most likely to experience job enrichment and others likely to be prepared for changing jobs and receiving new training. Also, leaders, responsible for these changes and the welfare of their employees, HR-representatives and psychologists etc. should be engaged.

Together they represent the team at this point in time. As a study-group they could, for instance, be able to discover ways of understanding and handling both the situation and people involved putting them in a position to direct the change.

5.4. Creating team events

The previous chapter illustrated why it is necessary to specify team membership combined with the focus on a specific team event. When specifying and organizing such an event you can ask typical questions.

Questions for planning a team event:

1. What will be the focus of the team event?

2. Which people should be part of the team event?

3. Who (should) contribute to this focus? Are those players available?

4. Are there players who are experienced regarding this focus and do they have adequate communication skills?

5. If they have not been defined as part of the team so far, should they be invited? Are they needed right now?

6. Is there a shared understanding of roles and responsibilities regarding the outcome the event is designed for?

7. Are those involved who carry the necessary power themselves or have access to the decision makers?

8. Is there a shared understanding of roles and responsibilities regarding contolling and monitoring the event?

9. Is there a need for facilitators or observers to help clarifying, specifying and learning?

10. What is the role of internal and external providers of services?

5.5.   The team-event triangle

The team-event triangle is a didactic model understanding the controlling of team events better. It is designed to support professionals in organizing themselves and the team event.

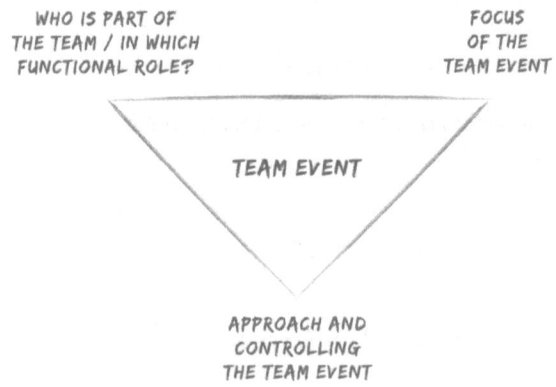

Fig. 13:   Team event triangle (Schmid 2004)

The triangle has 3 components (cf. Fig. 13 above)

1) focus of team event – For which purpose or goal should the team get together at this point?

2) members of the team – who should be included in the team at this point? In which roles and concerning which responsibility related to the set focus should they be engaged?

3) approach for monitoring the team event – which approach is appropriate from the perspective of those controlling and facilitating the event?

The focused responsibility of the team should match the individual's responsibilities according to their present roles in the team. Team observers and facilitators are able to focus on clarifications among the (potential) team members using this triangle. They may need to develop a shared understanding of the team's purpose, questions to be answered in an iterative process before and during the event. Facilitators may provide a learning framework for the team members and help them co-operate as a system. In order to accomplish this, leading and monitoring the team are usually handled as separate internal responsibilities.

Please be aware that the above said is meant to merely clarify perspectives and underlying ideas of the team event. Important skills and their practical use following pragmatic approaches are described elsewhere.

5.6. Vertical teams

The isb- definition of team implies that leaders and members of different structures within or outside an organization may be part of a team whenever they are part of a focused responsibility system. However, most people still think more "horizontally", when addressing "teams". One reason is the habitual preference to meet as a "horizontal team" e.g. directors on the same level or HR business partners with similar functions. Nevertheless, it might be more important to meet others with complementary responsibilities regardless of their hierarchical level. However, in these meetings those at eye level sharing responsibility might feel less comfortable than being amongst peers.

The following example illustrates considerations that speak in favor of defining "team" specifically for a particular event. It also demonstrates the transformation into a team event what usually is designed to be a bigger process, simply for numbers of people affected.

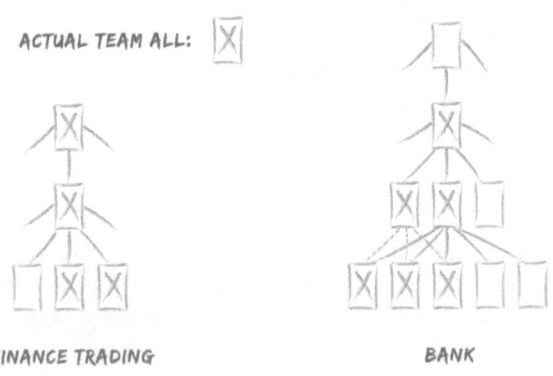

Fig. 14: Example: Arranging a vertical team event
(Schmid/Hipp 1998)

In Fig. 14 the structure on the left represents a medium-sized company being successful in trading with modern finance products. The structure on the right represents the part of a traditional bank having bought a trading company in order to integrate its expertise. In both companies, the customer services being the lowest level in both structures are assigned to work together towards this goal, but with no success. With rare exceptions, both sides kept sticking to their usual business and structures. The trading company continued selling modern finance products whereas most of the bank's customer service people did not manage to learn how to promote these products, thus failing to integrate the new knowledge into their work. Several explanations were offered explaining the cause, however, no shared and valid ideas were found to act on.

A vertical team workshop was arranged studying the situation in order to find out whether a solution exists and how both organizations should change to achieve this goal. If within this study-group workshop no solution was found selling off the trading company was considered an option. Serving this focus, team members for the meeting had to be selected. In order to represent the trading company, two members from the lowest hierarchy level were invited, one of them having managed to co-operate actively and the other having either failed with his partners or stayed passive so far. At this stage, it was unclear how the situation should be handled through the leadership chain up to the former executive of the trading company as contractor of the deal. The leadership chain on this side of the co-operation seemed not to have served the mission, even though understood as essential for a sustainable co-operation. Thus, middle and top-level leaders of both sides were invited, too.

From the bank side, three account managers were invited one of them having learned and integrated expertise into his daily business and a second colleague generally competent and interested, however, having failed to learn and integrate. A third colleague simply refused to co-operate. Further participants were their boss as well as somebody at the same hierarchical level. Both shared leadership with regional account managers bearing regional responsibility for the project (kind of matrix management). Finally, there was their boss at the higher hierarchy level having negotiated the bank's merger.

At this point in time, a total of ten team members were selected bearing in mind that this team might change due to the altering focus over time. Due to clarifications beforehand, this team was briefed concerning the overall situation as which as the methods to be used when setting up the team meeting.

5.7. Task and relationship orientation

Group dynamics and other approaches focus on two dimensions, i.e. task orientation and relationship orientation. Relationship orientation refers to experiencing relationships as to whether (a) people treat each other in a respectful and sensible way and (b) the organization deals with relationship problems as potential improvements of players positively resonating to each other.

Task orientation refers to content and outcome, i.e. in structuring and organizing task-fulfilling processes. For a performance team it is important to sufficiently focus on task orientation, as the reason since its existence is primarily performance. Nevertheless, relationship orientation is also essential for the welfare of a performance team as it helps creating meaning for people involved, especially fulfilling their basic need to belong, to influence others and to get personal resonance – all these points count for most human beings.

Both orientations matter and should be brought into specified balances. If one orientation dominates at the expense of the other, the result may be an unconscious subversive and immature dominance by the neglected orientation. Agitation with little real goal orientation and sheer group dynamics may dominate team life, ultimately damaging both relationships and performance. Group dynamics as an educational approach often follows the purpose of studying such polarizations, thus creating awareness and learning how to handle these two orientations. But essentially, one might turn to carefully designing and directing a performance-oriented group, i.e. building team culture.

5.8.   From group dynamics to team culture

For many years, operating professionally in team development was a domain of psychologists working with approaches of group dynamics. This approach was derived mainly from traditions of social psychology, psychoanalysis and sociology of groups. However today such approaches are only interesting as specific study groups in these disciplines. It is questionable whether the term "group" is specific enough a designator in most of these contexts. Group representing a rather socio-psychological focus is quite unspecific. Instead, using the term "team" as described before is appropriate. Although group dynamic programs are still on the market, for developing teams or qualifying professionals in teams in the field of organizations they are no longer considered as appropriate by the isb. This discussion in itself usually generates a lot of dynamics. The isb point of view is elaborated elsewhere (see Merkliste Chapt.5).

6.   Sharing professional competence

"If you want to walk fast, walk alone. But if you want to walk far, walk together." (Ratan Tata)

6.1.   What is competence?

Acting competently in an organization means to successfully contribute to accomplishing goals, to care for the system and to further develop the path for both. It is not surprising that success has a different meaning for everybody in different systems and under different conditions. Still there are people who are usually more successful than others in more different systems and under more different conditions. They are therefore considered more competent. But competence can only to some extent be attributed to individuals. Competence is mostly a matter of matching between an individual and an organizational system. Nobody can be competent in it without the others. Everybody has experienced people reenacting their personality in almost all surroundings and roles. There are individual talents, competencies and patterns of personality that sustain. For this part, increasing one's individual competence and developing one's personality by individual learning is the way to progress. On the other hand, everybody has experienced that - in spite of being the same person - we have different ways of experiencing and behaving in different contexts. Professionals have to organize themselves in the power field of an organization. And if circumstances are chaotic, it is difficult to stay clear and focused and if the situation is conventional and slow, it is difficult to interact in a dynamic and creative way. That is why increasing competence in interplay with others, organizing shared learning is a second way to move forward.

The ability of systems to design their own way of learning to-gether, developing a learning culture, let it be called systems learning, is a third way ahead. When providing a combination of the increasing individual competence, the competence of a system and the development of a learning culture, the situa-tion becomes ideal. The way in which individuals and systems can contribute to a shared learning culture will be discussed in the following chapter.

6.2.   Individual and organization

When discussing competence as quality shared between indi-viduals and organizations, it is helpful to clarify to what extent each side should be considered. Dimensions of an individual life must be limited to what can be accessed within the frame of an organization. Dimensions of an organization, however, must be limited to what is relevant for the individual in a given situation.

Fig. 15:   Encounter Individual – Organization (Schmid 2017)

Fig. 15 indicates that organizational roles define the area of relevant dimensions for both the individual and the system. There are other important aspects on both sides that are not or rather should not be considered at this point. For instance, discussing competence in organizations means discussing role competence in relation to the role structure of the whole organization. Questions around roles have been discussed in chapter 2.

Exploring deeper, Fig. 16 expands on the encounter between individual and organization. The organizational role requires a core expertise of an individual based on a professional identity standing for the core activities of that individual. Ideally, the organizational role as seen from the standpoint of the individual is identical with the function defined by the organization. Roles and core activities of individuals are clearly related to functions and core processes in an organization. As this ideal usually differs from reality, there is a permanent need for clarifying.

Here once again the mutual dependency between individual and organization becomes clear. Thus, individual development and organizational development together create personal competence within the interplay of organizational roles. At the same time questions of Organizational Development have to be discussed.

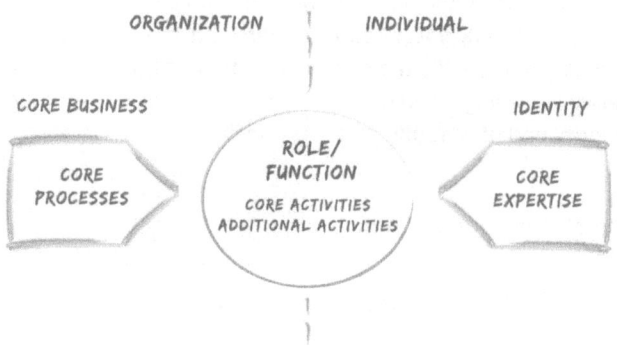

Fig. 16: Individual roles and Organizational function
(Schmid/Messmer 2003)

6.3. Competence of individuals

To consider individual competence and to identify necessary developments the isb Formula I "competence for individuals" (see Fig. 17) has proved useful.

The formula defines competence as composed by role competence, context competence and matching personality.

Thus, three basic questions are illustrated:

1. Are you capable of playing the role assigned to you in the play?
2. Do you understand the play in which you will play the role?
3. Do the requirements concerning your role and contribution to the play fit with what has meaning for you including other dimensions of your personal life?

Using the metaphor of a soccer player, becoming competent in defense, you should learn all the techniques of a defense player. Beyond that, you need to understand the logic of playing defense in a specific team as well as its strategy. Furthermore, defense playing should match with your talents, ambitions, identity and philosophy in sports and life.

The isb Competence-Formula I:

Fig. 17: Competence for individuals (Schmid 2008)

The outcome of Formula I is generated through multiplication illustrating that if one dimension is low it diminishes the impact of the other two significantly. In the case of the competence as a leader, your impact diminishes if you understand your organization but do not learn how to lead, or, although being an experienced leader, you do not understand the logic of the field you are in. Or perhaps you may even know how to be a leader and understand the system, but you and your organization have been developing into different directions causing loss of trust into each other. On the other hand, in Formula I limited compensation is possible. As a highly passionate leader you may inspire others a lot even though your competencies concerning roles and context still require further development. Looking at this formula will help detect which choice of context and role applies, which kind of learning fits and in what area development is most effective.

6.4.   Competence of systems

The competence of a system is defined through 1. coordinated individual competencies, 2. a shared learning culture and 3. matching and imbedding both into the organization's business and development, considering its relevant environment. (see Fig. 18)

The isb Competence-Formula II:

Fig. 18:   Competence for systems (Schmid 2013)

Formula II again is illustrated by building up the competence of a soccer team.

To begin with, each player must be a talented and skillful soccer player. However, these individual competencies have to be combined to build team competence. Thus, teams as such have to be constantly trained striving to sustain and raise their competence. Whether or not the efforts are successful depends on the quality of building both a common philosophy and a daily practice of learning together (cf. next chapter). However, in the end success depends on the co-ordination of the developing world of soccer in different dimensions. Obviously, a system's competence cannot be developed simply through individual training.

6.5. Matching

When considering competence improvement, individual learning should not be overemphasized. Beyond the system's effect of learning explained above, matching is important. Let's say you are a rather introverted person tending to be slow, but good at long-term systematic work dealing with a challenge. You watch out to only interact with others whenever you see a real benefit in it, preferring not to present results until you have reached a level you find satisfying. You may find yourself not performing so well working in an extraverted business making you feel rather distracted and stressed (cf. chapter 11.11.). In such organizations, things are supposed to move fast and provisional, constantly in interaction and coordination with others. In an effort to increase your performance and satisfaction, you might learn to adapt to a certain extent, however, this may prove not to be as efficient and effective or quite strenuous for your type of personality.

Improvement through personal learning may be desirable but considering the matching between the individual and the organization may be more fruitful. Better matching initiated by either the individual or the organization can lead to improvements being more easily achieved. At the isb, professionals often try to raise their competence and performance mainly by personal training, while clarification and actualization of matching with their organization might turn out as much easier and more successful. If feeling uneasiness in your organization, tending to blame either yourself or your organization is common. In reality, each of the two sides may well be ok individually, but just do not fit well together. In other cases, matching might be lost over time through incompatible developments. As we learned from the competence formulas earlier, compatibility is also a question of meaning. Fig. 19 invites us to check our matching in this dimension from time to time.

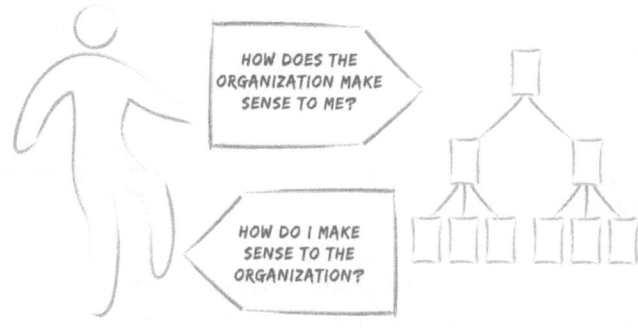

Fig. 19:   The Matching of a Human Beings and an Organization
(Schmid 2013)

Questions for clarifying matching (examples):

4.   Is the individual's core competence needed and welcome in the function she/he is currently performing or is going to perform?

5.   Does the expected task, lifestyle of work and prospective development matter to the organization? Are there meaningful career paths?

6.   Does the individual have the passion and the competence to contribute to the core business and the business development of this organization?

7.   Do possible functions and career paths offer the individual the prospect of identity sufficiently attractive to really become part of the organization?

While initially formulated from the individual's perspective, these questions should also be asked from the organization's side. If the answer to any of these questions is "No", further clarification or at least a checking agreement from time to time is required.

Only the right key can open the lock - with the wrong one all the effort is wasted.

Let us take the case of a young psychologist, who had expertise in the use of modern media. He was hired to develop IT support and media for a training institute. However, somehow this function did not satisfy his extroverted side, i.e. his talents and ambitions in presenting himself to audiences.

This mismatch caused conflicts as he appeared to overemphasize the importance of public attention to his ideas. Thus, he felt disappointed and doubts about competence arose, causing extensive talk about matching and options. As changing his function within the organization was not possible, he was offered a new co-operation contract as freelance seminar facilitator.

This change sparked an astonishing development sustaining his self-esteem and keeping good relationships to his former organizational environment.

Let us revisit our example of vertical teams in Chapter 5.6. Remember there was a merger between two organizations, expecting that the individuals were supposed to somehow learn from each other. In cases like this it may turn out that even the new job profile does not match the development potential of some individuals involved. Some may not have the kind of personality while others may simply not be able to give a meaning to the new expectations. This is where clarifying matching beyond pure training is essential. As an outcome, the architecture of the merger may be discussed, rather than forcing everybody into mismatches.

6.6.   Optimal role model distance

Individuals or systems deciding to engage with each other should consider in which dimensions they are similar and in which they are rather different. Finding a balance between "birds of a feather flock together" and "opposites attract each other" is essential. Far from offering straight advice in this matter, let us suggest an optimal distance between partners with different qualities to co-operate and learn from each other. It is fruitful for each partner to be ahead in different dimensions, acting as role models for each other. If there is maximal role model distance to a desired partner, this may leave the inferior partner to escape into either withdrawal or idealization and dependency rather than developing an eye-level relationship. In this case both sides will not be actively contributing to learning from each other, turning into positively critical partners. On the contrary, the relationship of sharing and co-evolution breaks down, even leading to some subversive dynamics. If there is minimal matching distance there might not be enough attraction and benefit learning from each other and seeking each other's respect. Thus, ideally there should be adequate role model distance between partners inspiring each other in order to reach out for the other's competences and complementing them.

6.7.   Maturity

The word "mature" is sometimes misinterpreted as "being of value". Here the term maturity is used in the sense of "being ready for". If you set out to climb a challenging mountain, you should be experienced and well-prepared regarding equipment, conditions, weather, food and drink supply, and even considering cases of emergency. If you are not ready or mature enough for such an adventure, you may easily experience stress, frustration, failure or even serious danger. In spite of obvious similarities with individuals and organizations, there is usually not enough clarity about the validity of these points for professional or organizational enterprises.

Programs for increasing competence often do not meet the expectations, as the gap between starting level and the target level of the intended development step is too big. In training and supervision in particular, participants often expect almost to get catapulted to an intended level no matter how appropriately estimated the base line or the necessary invest may be. Some companies also tend to expect change processes based on unrealistic expectations.

The story about horse jumping (cf. Chapter 4.1) may help illustrate the interplay between the maturity of a professional player and the "organizational horse" that is to be ridden. If neither the particular professional nor the system is experienced in the intended performance and competent in learning, the way to reach a higher competence level may turn out to be longer and more challenging than expected.

If only the professional is at a low level of maturity, the learning process can be concentrated on individual learning preferably related to the present task within the organization. If the level of maturity is generally high, the learning process can be concentrated on understanding the system's experience, one's own maturity, available resources and learning opportunities. Unfortunately, we often find both sides, i.e. the individual and the organization are at a low level of maturity, without being aware of this and unprepared to face this reality.

Bringing this into awareness and designing realistic steps towards raising competence at all levels is a delicate task. The paradox is that a certain level of maturity is needed for even understanding and accepting the present level of maturity and defining requirements for its sustainable growth. However, the usual dilemma is that the more immature the system is the more illusionary ideas on requirements and on quick and easy growth tend to be about.

6.8.   Maturity of Protagonists

You want find out which competence you can make use of and what the chances are for the necessary learning, you need an analysis of the maturity level of the individuals involved.

Thus, the isb introduces methods of maturity analysis before a study group organizes a learning process for a particular protagonist. During the assessment the protagonist is invited to give a first brief outline, i.e. a brief activity description of a few minutes, of the project he/she is involved or wants to be. In order to gain an educated guess about the protagonist's maturity, the learning partners should actively ask some questions.

Questions for exploring maturity:

1. *What is your task, your role and your responsibility in this project?*

2. *How is your task, assignment, responsibility, qualification and availability related to the other players involved?*

3. *To what extent are your ideas already a shared reality with others involved?*

4. *Do you have sufficient access to those who are in charge?*

5. *Do you know enough about their intentions and the history of the project?*

6. *What experience do you have with this kind of project?*

7. *What is the experience of your organization with projects of this kind and size?*

8. *How realistic is the organization of the project and the readiness to realize it?*

9. *Would the organization tolerate necessary adaptations?*

10. *What is your personal experience of learning in this field and with the learning approaches provided here?*

A maturity checklist for individuals (cf. below) focuses on gathering the impressions that could be gathered about the maturity of an individual. Its dimensions should best be kept in mind when dialoguing about goals, attitudes, approaches and responsibilities in the intended process out there and in the learning-process starting right here and now.

At this stage, we hope to share at least intuitively the reality of the project which results in a convincing mutual agreement. This serves as a sound basis for any further clarifications necessary to prevent disappointments in the subsequent learning process.

Maturity check list for individuals:

The individual

1. is able to outline the project of the organization and his/her status.

2. can communicate comprehensible images of roles and functions.

3. has a realistic assessment of abilities and responsibilities of the people involved.

4. has an idea of necessary contracts and responsibilities concerning the project and his/her role.

5. actively develops ideas about necessary clarifications, resources and procedures.

6. is able to explain the organization in a way that it gives an impression of its maturity.

7. is experienced with projects of this kind and is taking care of his/her own support. Knows what kind of support he/she needs.

8. contributes to the project (and the maturity check exercise) in a fact-based way, stays focused and resonates on feedback adequately.

9. is open to constructive criticism and contributions to the organization and is aware of his/her fallback positions, in case clarification in the organization should fail.

10. maintains direction for his/her plans and the learning process, thus constructively shaping the learning relationship.

6.9. Maturity of Organizations

The maturity checklist for organizations (cf. below) focuses on collecting impressions about the maturity of the organization. The main steps are establishing a discussion with the protagonist on the maturity of the relevant parts of the organization, and conclusions to be drawn for reaching goals and learning. The fact that we can never speak to a system as a whole but only to observers inside and outside the organization, with different perspectives, contributes to the quality of the maturity dialogues that are essential for realistic assessments. In the study groups at the isb as well as in learning settings within organizations, describing maturity is a process going through individual 'bottlenecks' of those who report.

Therefore, the maturity of the individual or the organization sometimes remains unclear, leaving us to focus predominantly on the task of how to nevertheless come to a useful judgment.

Maturity check for organizations:

1. Is the organization experienced with projects of this kind and size?

2. Where do we find access to relevant experience?

3. Is the system both able and ready to learn from mistakes?

4. Is there enough clear reality for the project to be shared? Do the relevant people have realistic ideas?

5. Are the necessary resources available? Is clarification possible? If not, would we be in a position to question the project?

6. Do actors have sufficient competences and ideas concerning their own contributions and responsibilities? Is planned manpower really available?

7. Is the project sufficiently supported by the power structure? Can support be ensured throughout the project?

8. Is there the willingness and competence to deal with conflicts that may arise? If not, who will pay the price?

9. Is there clarity about who will evaluate progress and results? Does evaluation lead to reasonable consequences?

10. Generally speaking, does the project make sense, and if not, can it be discussed?

These maturity check questions are not limited to examine the maturity level itself. However, they can be expanded to planning or contracting. Derived conclusions are to be discussed within project groups or study groups.

Questions exploring consequences of maturity:

1. How realistic are the chances for the organization to accomplish these goals?

2. How well can the protagonist position himself/herself?

3. How can the protagonist improve dialoguing on responsibility?

4. What can be done right now and in the medium term?

5. If any ambitions of organization or protagonist cannot be met, can they be adjusted?

6. Which alternative options can be suggested under current conditions?

7. How can players protect themselves and others?

Whether and to what extent a professional and an organization are ready for maturity checks and maturity dialogues is a major criterion for the state of maturity itself.

7.   Sharing Learning

"Learning culture" is a container term defined as the part of culture (see Chapt. 12) dealing with learning. Container terms give an immediate feeling of knowing, although there are diverse perspectives and procedures, which have to be identified, selected and integrated. Looking at learning culture means looking at structures, processes, experiences, behaviors and ventures from the perspective of learning. It is a specific perspective which focuses on learning as perspective complementary to such as finance, leadership, effectiveness etc.

Learning culture in an organization covers philosophy, policy and daily practice of learning. It has to do with programs, investment, the style and quality of communication, attitudes etc., all summarizing the way learning is handled in this organization. Learning culture clearly goes beyond the sum of individual learnings, even though it is the individual in whose behavior and experience it becomes apparent.

Examples of components of a high-quality learning culture

On the part of the teachers:

1. **didactic responsibility**: teachers have a plan and suitable procedures for the implementation in the learning processes

2. **personal authority** in the guidance of learning processes: teachers credibly and personally stand up for the content and values conveyed.

3. willingness and **ability to meet**: teachers engage in personal encounters with the learners.

On the side of the learners:

4. **focus discipline, role discipline, time discipline**: everyone disciplines themselves to fulfil the roles agreed for a learning setting, to follow the topic and to adhere to the time schedules.

5. willingness to **learn in partnership**: everyone contributes their own learning concerns, assumes responsibility for learning together and supporting others.

6. willingness to **resonate**: everyone offers others honest and tactful feedback reflection on the current status and upcoming developments.

On the part of the educational organization:

7. **program responsibility**: organizational processes and the contributions of teachers and other co-designers together form a program that is beneficial for learners.

8. **transparency and willingness to engage in dialogue**: dialogue on programs, procedures and behavior is held constructively and at eye level between all parties.

9. **adherence to appointments**: appointments are not only in form, but also in meaning. Changes require active new appointments.

10. **communication reliability**: everyone assumes responsibility for ensuring that others are adequately informed and that communication is satisfactorily concluded.

7.1.   Learning and working

In creative jobs, work tends to be a mix of little repetition and a lot of new creation. To a great extent, work can be defined as a process of learning. Consequently, organizing and developing work means organizing and developing learning. To develop individual competence oriented towards real work, many components and approaches have to be integrated. Nevertheless, in the mind of most people working and learning are still treated as two separate planets. In consequence, connecting learning and work remains an additional task. Alternatively, we suggest that developing work, professional learning and developing organizations "share one planet", i.e. joining forces with modern learning cultures such as integrated cultures of schools, companies and other organizations.

7.2.   The Dual System

In Germany there is a long tradition "dual education", i.e. combining classroom and workplace learning. Students attend schools or seminars undergoing classroom learning while at the same time developing job skills and learning at their workplace. Thus, they contribute practical perspectives to classroom learning and bring in knowledge from their departments, companies and require practical training, also in the light of the challenging jobs. This requires classroom learning to provide an understanding of real challenges concerning current issues, co-operating with real partners and creating applications in their day-by-day reality. Although the didactics of both learning settings are not always directly related to each other, it is worthwhile finding out to what extend classroom learning leads to better work in professional and organizational roles, and to which degree work practice enriches and challenges classroom learning.

7.3. Change in paradigm

Nevertheless, Germany is still widely tied to old habits of learning culture. Their paradigm about learning has always been that content comes first, and only then the learning of individuals or systems and a subsequent creative application in a variety of contexts may happen - if it happens at all. The task of transferring knowledge into application-related situations, integrating it with other complementary knowledge and implementing it into the learner's development and personality or into learning cultures specific to their fields is usually left to the professionals themselves. Yet the future of learning is switching that paradigm. Now learning culture comes as first priority, content follows in second place. Creative learning in application-related situations is becoming the main focus of a responsible learning culture.

The isb as a private academy actively engages in this necessary and ongoing paradigm change. For the isb rather than the focus on content challenges for systems and related individuals in different roles and teams in different real-life situations come first. Didactics closely applied to the challenges of work are developed, respecting a variety of individual learning conditions and individual styles, integrating them into each participant's competence portfolio. This learning design never aims to reduce learning to bare skills for specific applications. It raises the educational level, as it includes the understanding of principles and meaning by developing examples of reality. After all, the isb learning culture is designed to take personal development and education beyond the direct application achieved in dual learning.

Our effort aims at enriching learning systems integrating many components: the same people who work together should also learn together finding unique solutions to problems, continuously engaging in a shared learning frame, and getting used to a shared learning culture. While individual learning happens with reference to specific challenges, learning with others contributes to a learning community and its learning results. Furthermore, it encourages further shared and self-directed learning whenever this is needed. Content knowledge is still important. However, it is clearly second priority. First comes the understanding of how a lesson can be learned in a self-organized mode. Only then the question arises of which content should be inserted from which sources required. Nowadays everybody is facing an abundance of knowledge and content. What makes the difference is accessing, selecting, and shaping information. By and large, plenty of knowledge and talent are already present in a system in which there is a need for learning. But how is this information shared and transformed into the learning steps presently required? Most of the time, learning goes hand-in-hand with improving co-operation. Why not initiate learning between those who have to co-operate anyway?

It can be assumed that probably 90% of learning is achieved in a way not organized or accompanied by teachers or learning specialists. Therefor the remaining 10 % of learning happening explicitly can really only consist of examples. From learning processes around examples further self-organized learning has to be developed.

7.4. Individual and organizational learning

According to the discourse on professional competence (cf. chapter 6), shared learning in an organization means combining individual improvements within a specific organizational frame. Trying to replace organizational learning by a separated context of individual learning is both of limited success and exhausting.

Professional learning within organizations is an integrated day-by-day endeavor and a competent interplay characterized through three headlines:

1. Qualifying individuals with respect to systems

2. Qualifying systems with respect to individuals

3. Systems learning

7.5. Qualifying individuals

Qualifying individuals means qualifying them with respect to their talents, goals and the degree of professionalism reached so far in their learning history. Learning culture and its didactics should include these perspectives beyond just teaching contents and skills. By "respect to systems" we mean the qualifying of individuals in the light of challenges, roles and responsibilities within a particular organization. Learning culture and didactics should refer to the functioning of a team or the whole system, always related to their task and their particular style.

Looking at leadership qualification for instance, it makes a difference whether you come from an authoritarian or an anti-authoritarian background. It also matters whether you are leading a working group on a peer level in face-to-face-contact or whether you are acting with formal power exercised in virtual contact most of the time. It also makes a difference whether you are leading a winning team used to flexible and self-directed work, or whether you are leading a low performing team running the risk of being fired. If learning fails to take account of specific features of individuals and systems, there is little chance to improve leadership.

7.6. Qualifying systems

Qualifying systems means having an idea about what e.g. a department has to activate in order to function, and how it can be learned within a shared process. Learning culture and its didactics should understand the challenge and the gap between the status quo and target qualification required. Also, the structures, processes, and circumstances within which learning has to be organized have to be considered. When talking about "respect for individuals", we focus on their personalities as they are undergoing the intended learning processes. Do these personalities understand why they are doing something? Are they personally motivated? To what extent can they build on existing individual or shared learning experiences and skills?

Let us look at the example of vertical team development (cf. chapter 5.6) where a classic bank department is to be qualified for trading with modern banking products. It makes a difference whether the necessary facilities, working time arrangements, knowledge about products, accessible IT-support, consulting skills and material are available or not. Additionally, it matters whether there is a real chance for customers to actually develop an interest in the new products especially in view of the defined circumstances of change. However, the biggest difference derives from whether the employees assigned to the new products have the interest and the capacity to learn new roles, develop new identities, feel attracted by this kind of job enrichment including the prospect to receive credit for it. Are they ready to enhance their career chances, comply with the new challenges, and to work with one who is appropriate? If the improvement of a system is well designed, but does not respect the individual qualities available, the outcome for the organization might be disappointing.

7.7.   Systems learning

Intelligent open seminar learning is suitable for providing personal qualifications for individuals. Just how appropriate is it for qualifying teams? If there is a shared understanding about what people need to learn with respect to their roles in the organization and if there is a HR strategy to make that learning happen, individual learning is a good basis for developing a competent system. However, it is clear to watch for everybody how limited the effect is on direct improvement of teams, on undergoing necessary changes and OD, as well as on building up a culture of self-directed learning within the company. Here you need systems learning.

Systems learning is similar to learning new songs and new ways of singing in a choir in open seminars. If you send individual members of a choir to those seminars and they come back to their choir, yet still only little familiar with what they have learned, one can hardly expect to have the choir join them singing in this newly discovered way as well. If several choir members participate in the same training, chances are higher. However, if the whole choir - or at least a critical number of key-singers - are to learn something new together, chances are high the choir will sing in the newly discovered way. This is what we mean by the "systems-learning effect".

1. Systems learning combines qualifying people and qualifying systems in many ways. This is illustrated in Fig. 20

2. Systems learning comprises many aspects of learning described in this book. It includes various systemic mindsets, i.e. notions (leadership as either chain or network) or goals (building up a responsibility culture), structures (link between OD and HR department), processes (like starting "culture first" through examples) or values (sustainability achieved by caring about tasks and people) etc.

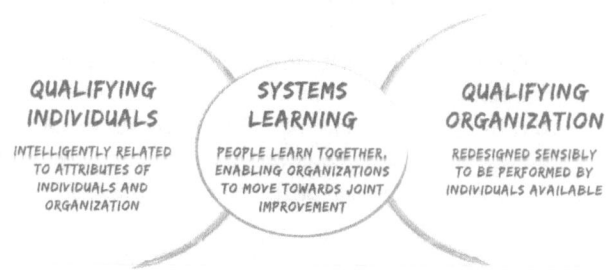

Fig. 20:   Systems Learning (Schmid 2017)

Aspects of systems learning:

1. Team Learning - those who share responsibility working together in the organization identify their learning requirements. They organize spaces for joint learning with initial support from facilitators if required.

2.   Learning within roles - in the learning process players adopt or keep their roles in a team or the organization. Roles focus on self-guidance, task orientation, and interplay with other roles.

3.   Task-oriented learning - examples from real tasks are used as material for learning. They should be of limited size so that learning is easy to achieve and attention to the learning process remains high. Task-oriented learning focuses on learning, not on task performance.

4.   Improvement of learning processes – while task-oriented learning is currently focused on performance, the team organizes retrospectives that reflect their learning process, both from an individual perspective and from the interaction as a system.

5.   Self-directed learning – team members learn to use methods and materials for learning, creating a self-directed, shared learning process. Some are only involved in being a competent member of a learning community, others in order to act as a peer facilitator.

6.   Learning and working – learning becomes part of everyday professional life and work culture. Whenever needed, explicit learning phases can be easily activated while working. Everyone knows how to switch between task orientation and learning orientation and actively integrate both into workflows.

7.   Multiplication of learning – these learning methods can be transferred to the entire organization at the peer level with the support of specialists. Typically, there will be a gradual process of dissemination of those who work directly together in growing circles.

8.   Building up a learning culture – this type of learning can be transferred to other departments through peer facilitation as an HR-strategy. Peer facilitators are familiar with their organization but do not directly share responsibility in a specific unit or segment. However, they may have similar challenges, roles, expertise, etc. in their respective departments.

9.   Job enrichment as an expert for learning – some professionals may discover passion for facilitating professional learning, either as part of their work in the organization or even in shifting their professional priority.

10.   Integration in HR strategy – the HR department is gradually taking on the role of mentor of all kinds of self-directed learning in balance with the adopted learning culture and integrating it with seminar learning and coaching. Seminar learning in open groups continues to include basic education for individuals according to their respective competence portfolio, as well as the learning strategy for all team members.

11.   Integration in OD strategy – HR specialists and people in charge of OD, change, leadership and organizational culture become partners who form task forces for the development of the organization.

12.   Networking as a learning organization – the learning culture is presented to the public as a competitive advantage and to local partners as a criterion for cooperation and mutual support.

7.8.   OD-Learning

There are some specifics for learning in the frame of Organiza-tional Development (OD), what we call OD-Learning. Each team development or OD process will face new challenges at different levels. In addition to new solutions to current prob-lems, there should be room for improvement in this learning process. Learning by example for further solutions and learning processes in an OD-process we call OD learning. Traditionally, not enough time and capacity is calculated for this type of (meta)learning, the development of learning beyond solving the problem. It is never easy not to prioritize the current prob-lem solving, but shift the priorities to the qualification of the (learning)system. It should be possible in spite of the everlast-ing pressure to find solutions immediately. The intended re-sults of each OD should consist of 50% solution of the current OD problems and 50% improvement and multiplication of OD learning culture.

7.9.   HR learning

Traditionally any training organized by HR meant organizing seminars and selecting and delegating people to participate. However, HR learning can go far beyond that. Classic trainers are often focused on content(s) rather than competencies that match the organization's standards of behavior and culture. In this way, you will be confronted with many "transfer prob-lems" because people have not been trained in easy-to-use behaviors or in a company-specific learning culture. They have never learned the same "learning-culture language" that al-lows them to easily share further learning. In addition to de-veloping fragmented skills, they also take on fragmented learn-ing cultures.

Differences in learning cultures need to be overcome if the interaction and learning within the organization is to be effective. HR often struggles with different terms, models, approaches, formats, beliefs, order of importance, and so on.

Inconsistencies and communication problems are often misinterpreted as content or relationship problems, even though they actually come from different approaches and learning styles. We are more likely to benefit from different individual learning styles and personalities while getting to know a common learning culture. However, differences in learning cultures can even be fruitful if well intentioned and facilitated.

Being an experienced learner and learning partner is a solid foundation of self-esteem. Some professionals even discover how talented they are as learning facilitators for others, and may be invited to participate in the learning cultures of their company. Some professionals include the role of a learning facilitator or organizational coach in their qualification portfolio. Some companies even include such qualifications into their job descriptions, creating an internal market for these jobs. For example, a German software company trains people to be qualified as coaches and learning facilitators beyond their traditional responsibilities. They can spend up to 10% of their total work on providing support and learning culture services in the company. This also supports cross-departmental learning within the company and provides another learning chance for the system.

7.10. External providers

If a company has a learning culture strategy that integrates the above-mentioned aspects of OD and HR learning, this would optimally influence resource conversation. The integration of a high-end learning culture is just as important for functionality and future orientation as the integration of a high-end IT system. The more the HR and OD departments are responsible and actually provide their services, the better for the company. When external providers are involved, it is important that they share the same learning culture. Sometimes big steps need to be taken, and it takes a lot of external staff to drive developments forward and make learning easier. Then, irritations can occur because they are not integrated or compatible with the existing learning culture. Additional providers should only be involved if they really share the learning culture right from the beginning and are thoroughly prepared and accompanied by "culture-insiders". The more these interns are willing to provide capacity, the more they can contribute to beneficial co-operation. Some external education systems, such as the isb-qualified systems learning, use specific open curricula in order to provide the expertise to build such a learning culture within organizations. In external or internal curricula, they offer learning islands, exemplary of the region to be fostered. Fig. 21 shows this idea. The curricula of the isb academy are conceived as islands on which participants can qualify as experts in establishing corporate learning cultures and become part of a network with others doing the same.

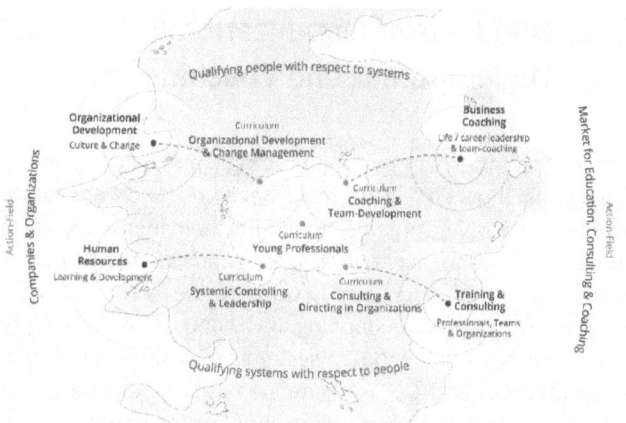

Fig. 21: isb a learning island

8. Mindsets of Organizational Development and Coaching

In recent decades, Organizational Development (OD) and Organizational Coaching (OC) have become major approaches towards developing organizations and their members. In this area, some fashions have developed, which sometimes do not match with the isb approach. In order to clarify this, we would like to explain our understanding of OD and OC in this chapter. In accordance with all modern systemic approaches, we do not understand OD and OC as predefined sets of tools and solutions. We understand both as a bundle of descriptions, attitudes, ways of thinking, approaches, styles, and organizing events. Consequently, it is not the setting, concept or tool which determines whether OD or OC match with the isb approach. We do not invest in exaggerated uniqueness and polarization, but rather accept a wide range of reasonable approaches. And we offer our understanding to facilitate comparisons and connections. We endorse the saying that "it is not the hammer that makes the artisan, though a hammer may be more or less useful for a particular use!"

As explained in chapter 5, we describe organizations as consisting of individuals in their organizational roles, each having their own understanding of the organization. Their understanding reality and organization is essential to the organization's performance, development and culture. That is why dialogue with people is important. What should be conveyed must overcome the bottleneck of dialogues, if necessary. If these bottlenecks are blocked or too tight, only schemata and emotions remain.

8.1. Dialogic OD

Definition: The isb defines OD as the evolution of human systems for the current and future performance of an organization. "Dialogic" means "through communication" between those who act as the organization together. Dialogic OD means OD through communication. The label "Dialogic OD" was introduced by Gervase Bushe and Robert Marshak. They compare it to "Diagnostic OD", i.e. a label for approaches, which introduce solutions to an organization from the outside. Based on a modern way of thinking that we would call systemic, Bushe, Marshak and their co-authors create a theory and practice of OD that focuses on dialogue, yet allowing the integration of many classic, popular, and successful OD approaches. While sharing most of their ideas, the isb approach has been independently developed and published. Below is a brief overview that gives an idea of isb 's systemic thinking and approaches:

8.2. isb-perspectives of OD

8.2.1. Focusing on people

OD means the development of human systems. As described in chapter 5, the definition of the organization depends on what an observer is focused on. When you focus on structures and processes, you tend to put them in the foreground and the people in the background. The isb is focused on people who run an organization, so on their roles and responsibilities, their competencies and behaviors. Structures and processes are subjected to these dimensions and their interaction with human participation in reality is seen as essential.

8.2.2. Link to cultural development

OD is inevitably linked to Cultural Development (CD) as the way people organize and interact is essential. The conscious and unconscious ways as well as the rules for co-creation are what we mean by culture (cf. chapter 12). The behavior of people can neither be understood nor really be influenced without acknowledging the individual and the collective culture. It is therefore obvious that systemic OD is generally also CD. Cultural dimensions cannot be ignored if we create newly lived realities.

8.2.3. Principles, attitudes and perspectives

OD is defined by principles, attitudes and perspectives rather than by "how-to formulas". If we look at the multitude of possible situations of OD, schematic solutions obviously will not fit well. People need to find their own solutions within defined frameworks that are applicable to a variety of options. Principles, attitudes and perspectives give hints how this can work and which options are available. Specific descriptions can never be sufficient, as they are only examples of important principles which provide orientation.

Some prominent rules which offer a taste of the isb cultural orientation:

1. Define **frameworks** and clarify the **contracts** with owners. Make clear that they are responsible and how long in the process their support is needed. Too many fires die out after being launched as a straw fire.

2. Consider the **maturity levels** of individuals and organization (cf. chapter 6.7.). Avoid the temptation of jumping further than you and your horse are prepared to do.

3. **Reduce the complexity** to a tolerable and controllable minimum. Introduce simple but never oversimplified dialogues on measures to take appropriate steps in the right direction.

4. Tolerate as **few greenhouse effects** as possible. Greenhouse effects may provide seduction but typically raise unrealistic expectations and allow frustration to those who try to repeat things under outdoor conditions. Disappointment through illusions can leave scorched ground behind.

5. Organize yourself as if you were preparing for an **endurance run**. Be wise with energy, invest 1/3 in current performance, 1/3 in the upkeep of future business and 1/3 in your people.

6. Ensure **realistic timing and a step-by-step approach**. Building up a sustainable culture takes time and repetition that may seem endless. People learn more easily what they can do better in the near future.

7. Find your **balanced pace** like a tightrope walker between too fast and too slow. A certain pace may be optimal for the topic, but it needs to be adapted to the style of the organization and its service providers.

8. **Follow** your **cultural principles in all processes**. It is an illusion to believe that you can start to move quickly and bring culture later (cf. introduction). Note that "quick and dirty" usually stays dirty.

9. Build up a common understanding of your situation and intentions before you begin.

10. Discuss key facts and figures before you start.

Questions to be discussed on key facts and figures (examples):

1. What is the overall context we are starting within?

2. What are our main intentions?

3. How will our situation have improved after the project?

4. How can we create examples and experiments for further studies?

5. What are our main strengths and necessary learnings?

6. What shape are we in? Do we have reserve capacity?

7. How can we organize learning as we go along?

8. How can we integrate those who take responsibility in the end?

9. Are we realistic in our estimates of time, other resources, and conditions?

10. How and when will we include those, we need for the upcoming roll out?

Try to create examples for what the future should look like, organize prototypes as learning experiments and invite people to form "study groups". Choose steps which are useful to you if you need to stop the project. Choose an architecture that can be multiplied within the culture of the organization. Instead of experimenting with the whole system, develop a prototype that can be rolled out progressively as it works.

8.2.4. Methods for co-operating and learning

To serve the isb approaches, such OD and CD methods are used and illustrated, which support individuals, teams, and systems as well as actual behavior and further reality. All other approaches may be not economical, because of necessary efforts to translate and connect. As described in chapter 7, this is closely linked to shared learning. Other ways of describing organizational and other OD approaches can and should certainly be integrated, but stay in the background until needed.

Some methods of collaborative and shared learning have already been mentioned, such as dialogues on responsibility (cf. chapter 3), on maturity (cf. chapter 6.7), on competences (cf. chapter 6.3 and 6.4) and on matching (cf. chapter 6.5). Then there are team events of all kinds using the team-event triangle (cf. chapter 5.5). Especially in vertical teams (cf. chapter 5.6) the handling of leadership aspects (cf. chapter 4.8) is integrated. The isb offers a wide and rich repertoire of settings, methods, exercises, and tools as shareware many of which are written in English.

8.3. Hologram and spotlight metaphor

Nothing is as practical as a good theory (Kurt Levin). We certainly agree. Although the next chapters (8.3 -8.6) have serious implications for the approach to reality, they seem to be not easily accessible at first sight. If you feel this way, please feel free to continue with chapter 9. Our perspectives determine what we see. A rose is a rose is a rose. Agreed. And yet, a rose is something different when viewed by a gardener who thinks of the right soil, or by a child who wants to pick it without being hurt, or an ant that cultivates lice on this plant, or by a lover who wants to create an impression.

Basically, it is the same rose in each case, but at the same time different, taking into account the categories and interests that are determined by each approach.

Spotlight metaphor

At the isb, we use the spotlight metaphor to illustrate this. Perspectives are spotlights which focus on an object or an event. To get information, those spotlights should be chosen that show the differences that make the difference to what should be explored. You learn to understand and decide which spotlights make what difference. You learn to turn off unnecessary or irritating spotlights, destroying important contrasts by too much or the wrong light. It is neither necessary nor economical to have (too) many spotlights available or switched on at the same time. But you have to make intelligent decisions.

If you choose your spotlights on a habitual basis, you will not see anything else, even if you need it. You will learn to recognize which spotlights show you what you want to see and what not. And if you find that spotlights are missing, you can learn which new spotlights to install and turn on. You can combine spotlights in new ways to meet your specific interest, such as e.g. the gardener with the ant perspective on the rose, or the lover with the perspective of the child.

If you want a community to come up with new ways to handle something, you will need to replace spotlights and introduce new ones and install flexible power on and off capabilities.

The hologram metaphor

There is a well-known metaphor of several blind people approaching an elephant from different directions. It seems as if they are talking about different creatures, named the elephant. From a meta-perspective one understands why and from which perspectives this impression arises.

Using a hologram as metaphor provides the same insight, but in a more sophisticated way:

A hologram is a three-dimensional representation of any item. Take the human body looked at from all directions. Although all sorts of information are available, different perspectives produce different orders, depending on what we put into foreground and background. Information in the background stays there without being deleted, but being less focused. These concentrations vary according to the observer changing his position.

8.4.   Sharp contours and plausible cores

Professionals are often involved in unproductive discussions because they do not clarify what they are talking about. For example, board members want to decide whether team development can help to solve cooperation issues and should be part of the company's OD strategy. When they discuss this, they use ways to define things that do not lead to a common understanding. To improve this common understanding, a meta-model can help, that makes the definitions clearer and more useful.

In this concept, definitions with sharp contours are differentiated from those with a plausible core.

For reasons of scientific clarity, sharp-contoured definitions are more useful whenever the focus creates boundaries between the meaning of the terms to be distinguished. What belongs to term A cannot belong to term B at the same time. See Fig. 22.

TRAINING	ORGANIZATIONAL DEVELOPMENT
THERAPY	CONSULTATION

Fig. 22:   sharp-contoured definitions (example) (Schmid 2007)

However, for cultural purposes, plausible core definitions are more useful, as it is more important to understand meanings and to find descriptions, which give meaning to the essentials. For this benefit it can be accepted that terms overlap in their scope. See Fig. 23.

For example, if we apply this to the term "identity", self-images do not arise through differentiation, and certainly not through exclusion, but by collecting some of the characteristics of that identity. Other identities may partially claim the same characteristics.

When trying to distinguish psychotherapy from consultation, you may come across special exclusion criteria such as no "dealing with distortions" in consultation (A) or no "providing instructions" in therapy (B). In fact, some clients may show some aspects of mental disorder and the consultant has to deal with it. And therapy may be stuck due to lacking instructions, so that providing them may be therapy.

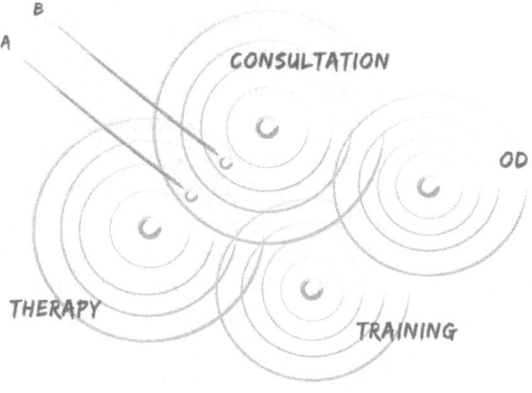

Fig. 23: topographical presentation of overlapping plausible-core definitions (example A= dealing with distortions B= providing instructions) (Schmid 2007)

Therapy and consulting should not differ so much in what is accepted or not, but in how things are dealt with and in which context they are imbedded. When therapists and consultants do not talk so much about limits but about typical aspects of their activities and their understanding of their effects, it is easy to understand their respective identities. Their overlap does not confuse their identity and competence, but creates opportunities for collaboration and recognition of the concerns of "neighbouring disciplines".

The tradition of sharp-contoured thinking is also one of the factors responsible for over-orientation in securing boundaries and the areas of competence. Figuratively speaking, too many resources are invested in "staking out and securing claims" instead of cultivating the land and filling the space.

Another cultural habit sometimes makes it difficult to represent identity individually and positively. We feel that we have to face a complete, homogeneous and non-contradictory description of an identity. Since this "uniform" rarely fits properly and every deviation must be justified, ambiguity and uncertainty about our identity are the result. We can welcome differentiating and sometimes polarizing comparisons with others as an enriching diversity. Only if we are not sure of our own identity, we try to gain a "firm" position for ourselves by polarizing with others. We need to give up a homogeneously professional understanding and see identity as a mosaic that has an essentially recognizable character and yet can appear in many variations. Thus, "plausible-core"-understandings of professions can be found with individual variations that do not claim exclusive characteristics in a colonialist way. There is hardly anything we can claim for ourselves exclusively. If we still believe that this is necessary to build a unique identity, we must deny others the quality that we claim for ourselves. Here an alternative construction can help, in which the distinctive character is recognized more by the particular combination of features than by the uniqueness of their components. It is this type of combination that makes a bunch of flowers unique, rather than claiming to consist of flowers that are not to be found in other bouquets.

8.5. Perspectives and events

The perspectives and events model provides a more practical framework for the ideas outlined in Chapters 8.3 – 8.4. It was developed to structure discussions about change and OD and to clarify the distinction between the focus on perspectives and the focus on events. (cf. the spotlight metaphor Fig. 24).

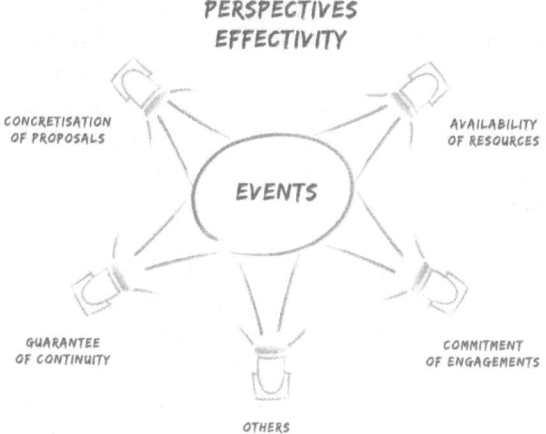

Fig. 24: Perspectives on events (spotlight-metaphor)
(Schmid/Messmer 2004)

Let us study the following example:

A: "We definitely need more effectivity in our project's cooperation!"

B: "I agree. I feel uncomfortable with our monthly collaborative meetings between the departments that share projects. Our monthly meetings should be rearranged."

A starts the discussion by emphasizing the perspective of "effectivity in cooperation". B responds focusing on the event "meeting". This can certainly cause confusion.

If we follow A's approach, the next step is to clarify what is meant by "effectivity", to define subcategories and the intended improvement. This can include things like 'concretization of proposals', 'guarantee of continuity', 'availability of resources', 'commitment of engagements' and others. Once the key underpinnings of effectiveness in co-operation have been clarified, it can be assumed which types of events or series of events need to be reorganized over time to realize improvement within those perspectives. The same perspectives can and should be applied to other events outside the monthly meetings.

B's approach would be to focus on a specific event, such as the monthly meeting, to generate ideas, why the meeting does not seem to be satisfactory, and what changes in the organization of the event could be considered satisfactory. The next step could be to discuss which changes best serve one or the other perspective. As a result, either the spectrum of perspectives for that event could be changed, or the event itself could be rearranged to the effect serve different perspectives.

Even if ultimately the same perspectives and events come into the focus of discussion, the decision whether to go the way through perspectives or through events is a strategic advantage.

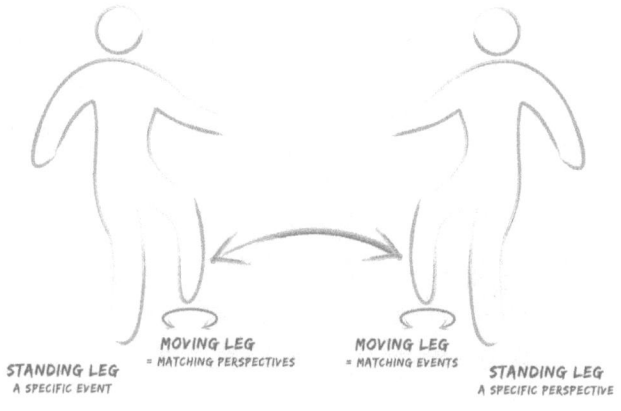

Fig. 25: Perspectives and events in two steps
(Schmid/Messmer 2004)

As shown in Fig. 25, walking requires both the "foot"-perspectives and the "foot"- events. So, we avoid starting with both legs at the same time or confusing them while walking, and we manage to move our feet in a coordinated way.

8.6. System solutions and five perspectives

Fig. 26 shows five major perspectives that are essential to considering whether an OD solution is valid. Please note that this selection is not theoretically rooted, but emerged from a resonant process of practical discussion that reflects errors in organizations. The diagram helps to clarify whether system solutions and OD projects refer to important differences in the 5 perspectives.

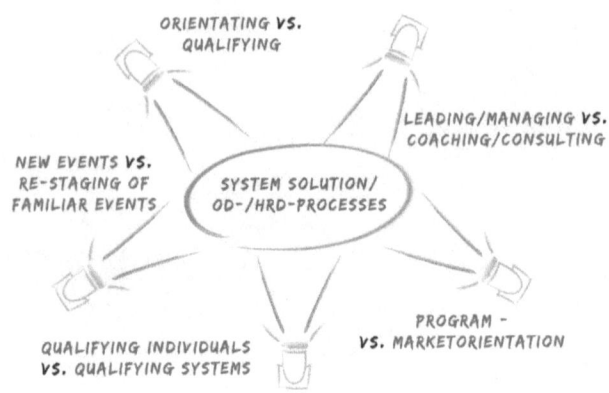

Fig. 26: Five perspectives on systems-solutions and OD-processes
(Schmid 2007)

Five major perspectives considering OD-solutions

1. *Is it qualifying systems or qualifying individuals?*

This difference has already been discussed in chapter 7.4. and
7.5. It is important to see how a qualification approach can be
focused on individuals so that the functioning of the system
improves at the same time, or that it aims to improve the system, but in a way that individuals can also learn a lot.

2. *Is it leading or coaching?*

We often find formal leaders who do not do their job but hire
consultants, a move that leads to an open or subtle shift concerning responsibility: the consultant tries to lead the process,
e.g. a team, while the leader denies his role and only gives

good advice. Neither of them can succeed as the process ceases to work as soon as difficulties arise. Make sure irritations are cleared in a timely manner.

3. *Is it professional qualification or organizational orientation?*

Often, workshops are offered to qualify people since organizational changes have not been successful. Closer examination may reveal that the people involved have no clear guidance on the intended changes, often due to the lack of sound development of the project. Even if there are skill deficits, a lack of strategic clarity cannot be offset by qualification. In this case, it is wise to insist on having support of internal staff with knowledge of the project the right to give orientation to others.

4. *Is it creating new events or rearranging given events?*

In times of intended change, managers often find ways of staging new events for whatever they want to improve. As a result, those affected are increasingly exhausted by these additional events. They often complain not to have enough time to do their regular work, let alone improve regular work according to the intended changes. While it is obviously easier to create a new event for each innovation, it is vital to master the truly necessary challenge to modifying given events in order to achieve the intended developments. The perspectives-event model (cf. Chapt. 8.5.) is useful as a tool for planning and designing this process.

5. *Is it oriented towards customer requirements or towards the provider's program?*

In principle every internal and external provider should be open to needs of customers. Often, however, external or internal providers have no clear orientation regarding what to offer at what level and how to meet those needs.

Some service providers simply go for what customers demand. When, for example, team workshops are commissioned, they follow exactly what the customer wants them to do. In one case, the focus is on facilitating communication in a team meeting, in other cases it is about directly dealing with team members on conflicts or providing coaching only for the team leader live or in separate sessions.

One thing is, what the costumer asks for, the other thing is, the providers policy what kind of services to offer. To substitute roles within teams requires a lot of capacity. In order to have larger effects with limited capacity, a program which challenges the team member's own competence might be more appropriate.

A provider's program may offer a basic training for team leaders in groups, teaching skills for leading their own teams, then organizing and facilitating further learning through peer supervision between team leaders, and only supervising them, when they are not working satisfactorily.

8.7. Organizational Coaching

Coaching is a "container term" covering all sorts of personal conversations designed to help people understand and manage their relationships, achieve goals, and lead a better life. Not every coaching concept or method is suitable for organizations. In many cases it is rather dealing with Coaching in a more general sense in the organizational field than with organizational coaching.

8.7.1. What is Organizational Coaching (OC)?

Organizational Coaches are decathletes!

Organizational Coaching focuses in particular on the relationship between individuals and their professional involvement in organizations. This relationship is the deciding factor for Organizational Coaching (OC). OC is always about learning, and coaches should be specialists in learning. Therefore, many aspects of OC have already been discussed in chapter 7.4. In OC, people are viewed through the eyes of the organization and the organization is viewed from the perspective of the individuals. Interactions between individuals and the organization are both the main interpretation framework and the development goal for OC.

As described in various chapters of this book, there are many specific perspectives that can be covered by the range of OC services. Many coaches prefer the one-to-one conversation as a setting and communication psychology as frame of reference. However, in OC this is only one choice out of many options. OC is interdisciplinary and organizational coaches are decathletes! The success of OC does not depend on acting on familiar perspectives (as psychology), but on the consideration and combination of many disciplines and aspects of leading organizations. While OC may be responsible for certain contractually agreed measures, OC also assumes responsibility related to the organization as a whole (cf. chapter 3.3).

8.7.2. Extended OC-Services

Let us look at some examples to get a feeling for more advanced OC services:

Coaching on "personal issues" ad libitum? When problems occur in the organization or its members, coaching is an accepted option today. Labelling something as a coaching issue usually implies the presumption that the problem belongs to someone, who is referred to as "coachee", and can be resolved by him or her with the help of a coach. For dispensing the organizations, coaching is supported somehow and it is up to the coachee to find a coach and solve their problems. Some companies establish coaching pools to ensure orientation and quality. These coaching pools range from simple lists of coaches to the definition of more detailed criteria and procedures.

In order to facilitate the choices in direction of organizational coaching, existing definitions and procedures under the contract should be reviewed.

Questions for reviewing possible Coaching:

1. What is defined as "the problem"? Who defines, who agrees, who asks questions whether the problem definition is appropriate and coaching is the right approach?

2. Who is interested in which solutions and who evaluates the results? Are these dimensions taken into account for a coaching contract between the coach, the coaching provider, the coachee and his organization?

3. Who should be involved and how will this be organized?

4. Does the coach's philosophy match the culture and style of the organization?

5. How is this coaching coordinated with the organization and any actions to be taken there?

6. Is there an HR strategy to build up competencies and clarify relationships between specific education programs, systems learning, and individualized teaching?

7. Is the coaching provider familiar with the requirements and options of the organization and is he or she willing to co-operate?

If OC is to improve competencies or career development, it should be clarified whether the target level can be reached in relation to the gap to be filled in time, whether all stakeholders are mature enough and whether the resources are available.

Specific Coaching programs

Many companies offer contingents of coaching sessions for specific steps, such as change roles, departments, or countries, etc. Here OD and OC may meet. For example, when there are assessments for a newly-launched change project or OD, then each aspirant could be given the opportunity to clarify questions around possible participation and matching in some OC sessions. A coaching contingent should be compatible with the type of coaching the coachee requests, but should also comply with the guidelines for the actual clarification step and the requirements of the project or OD.

In summary, the OC providers should be able to meet the specific needs of the coachee as well as the requirements of the organization. Advanced OC services require advanced OD and OC maturity for both the organization and the external providers.

8.7.3. Quality of OC Services

The examples above have shown that OC is not just an encounter between coach and coachee, but also between systems and programs. In chapter 6, competence was defined as a matching question. Following the same logic, the quality of OC has to match the programmatics of coach and coachee as protagonists of two organizations, i.e. two different worlds (see in Fig. 27).

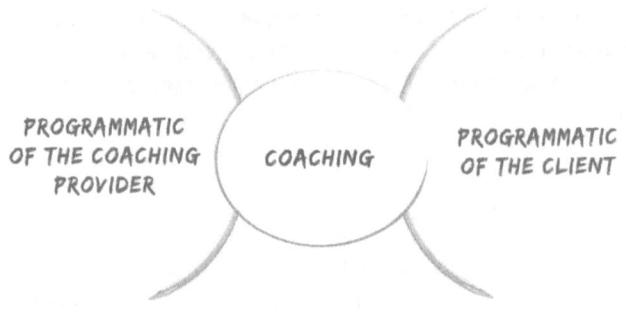

Fig. 27: Matching Coaching programmatics (Schmid 2016)

8.7.4. Expertise and professional perspective

OC is not necessarily connected with the role of a coach. Many professionals acquire coaching competencies without the clear goal of becoming a coach. Rather, they want to acquire expertise in the dimensions labeled OC to integrate those skills into other roles and services such as being a better team leader, or people-oriented OD provider. They want to improve as professionals enriching organizational culture from the perspectives of OC.

9. Sharing the crisis of coherence

9.1. What is coherence?

Coherence is a key term to individual and organizational health. There are many ways to describe a person or an organization as coherent. Coherence is for the isb described by "well organized" and "meaningful to the subjects" and the term is used as a synonym for integration. From the organizational perspective, these two components of coherence can be considered either low or high.

The organizational functioning gets low

Being well organized is essential for integration, especially when an organization has grown. This includes well-designed structures, a smooth interaction of processes, and the ability to grow in a complementary way. If the organizational functioning becomes too weak, this can lead to a crisis. When using a mechanical metaphor, loss of functionality means that the gears first reduce their locking more and more before some of the key contacts come loose. Despite even increasing effort the machine gradually loses its functioning.

Attachment to meaning gets low

Meaning is a fundamental integrating force. Even if some goals are achieved, coherence still diminishes when higher professional or organizational intentions become unclear. If meaning and purpose become too small, it can lead to a crisis. In other words, the machine may function well but lose the connection to its purpose or reason of being.

To put it in positive light: To stay coherent, an individual and an organization need a high score for the multiplication of "well-organized" and "meaningful":

This is illustrated by the following formula for coherence in profession and organization:

Fig. 28: Formula for coherence in profession and organization (Schmid 2018)

Not aspiring to a scientific definition of coherence, the metaphorical description should rather promote understanding and encourage the reader to apply it to his/her own reality.

When a professional or an organization loses coherence, there is a significant difference between what the causes of disorganization and loss of meaning. If there is a loss of being organized, this can be compensated by meaning and purpose and more engagement only to a limited extent. When meaning and purpose diminish, optimizing the organization can at least help to keep it functioning to a certain extent. In the first case you should start with the reorganization. In the second case, make sure you clarify, create, and share meaning and purpose.

Both factors can balance to some extent, but should ultimately be adjusted. In the long term, a highly meaningful company can suffer from inadequate organization and a well-organized company can suffer from lost meaning and purpose.

9.1. What is a crisis?

The term "crisis" is generally defined as "facing severe difficulties and reaching a turning point". A crisis can be perceived as a disaster or as an opportunity for development – the latter, only provided that the protagonists see the need and open up for major changes. In this particular context, crisis can be defined as a loss of coherence in a dimension that requires large movements either to reorganize or to generate new meaning and purpose.

The longer an impending crisis is ignored, the more problems arise which have to be solved immediately and simultaneously. Often problems even have turned into being insoluble and must therefore be understood and dealt with as dilemmas (cf. chapter 9.3).

In many situations, it is unclear whether they should be considered a crisis. Obvious difficulties are either not perceived or not considered essential, or it is difficult to identify criteria for diagnosing the situation as a crisis. Is the observed difficulty essential and drifting to a turning point or is it part of a standard variation? Do different players in organizations have the same experience, evaluation criteria and time perspectives?

9.2.   Phases of coherence crisis

Here a diagram is proposed to distinguish the phases of a crisis, providing a basis for both reflection on a crisis and dealing with reactions to it. The diagram shows the degree of coherence of an individual or an organization over time. The emergence of a crisis can be described in four phases which can overlap and be realized at different places at different times or differently by different protagonists. Typically, there is a time lag between realizing effects, identifying causes, reacting constructively, and observing the benefits of action.

Beyond professional life, this diagram can be applied to many areas, for example to health or climate change. Everyone has one's own characteristic relationship to every single phase of a crisis. There are certainly individual preferences and talents dealing with some phases, as well as irritation and missing awareness towards others. Dealing with these competences with regard to such tendencies means counting for some and discounting others (See also Fig. 29) A loss of coherence, (i.e. being well organized and meaning and purpose) results in disintegration:

Reintegration results in re-gaining coherence.

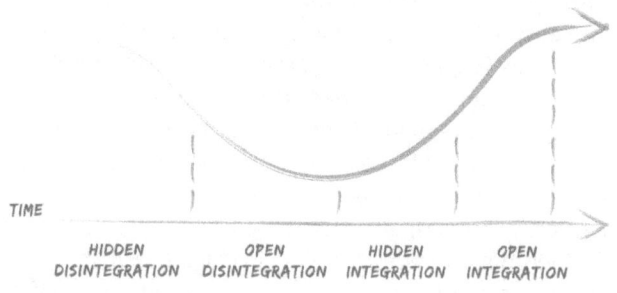

Fig. 29:   Four phases of crisis development (Schmid/Messmer 2004)

9.2.1.   Hidden disintegration

Internal and external requirements can often be subject of changes that are not recognized as significant by those responsible. This can lead to decay of all kinds without being aware of it, e.g. organizational failure, subtle losses of meaning and identity. At this stage of crisis, deviations of neither function nor purpose are considered relevant, causing hidden disintegration. Therefore, it is probably too early to consider a fundamental analysis of the situation, even though from an outside perspective this may be recommended. At this point in time, there are already some signs of a crisis behind the scenes, while confidence still prevails on the front stage.

9.2.2.   Open disintegration

As soon as problems last longer and reach more alarming dimensions, irritations become perceivable, a state we call open disintegration. But still more general doubts are hushed before unsettling the people in charge. Superficial judgments and activism, uncritical openness towards unrealistic solutions and investments in ineffective measures are tolerated without critical discussion, as long as "business as usual" remains untouched. It seems to be too early for a thorough analysis of the problems and for sound solutions, especially if this requires a change in habits. With delay and only slowly the ideas arise that business premises need to be questioned, and changes in structures, processes, and staff probably need to be considered. Then opportunities for less spectacular but more solid measures are considered, to be enacted by internal staff and proving useful every day.

9.2.3. Hidden integration

After more realistic judgments have been made and the right internal people have taken responsibility, useful programs run for some time, but there is still a lot of insecurity. Although solid actions have been taken, problems do not seem to be over yet. Although reasonable people are demonstrating their new ways of dealing with problems and people, thus expressing trust and appreciation, many aspects have yet to be clarified and put in order. Coherence is restored, though it is still hidden behind lasting disintegrations. It will take more time for things to stabilize, break up, and new tendencies to open up to a broader new reality. It is not easy to devote more time towards developing measures that have already been taken, but this time is needed to unfold effectiveness.

9.2.4. Open integration

Finally, things get easier as new processes work without any extra effort. People start to feel the relief, becoming calmer and more self-confident. Often, they are not even aware of this relief, because it has come so gradually. Experiences and attitudes have developed into habitual behavior, even without knowing exactly how this happened. Problems are dissolving or can be solved incidentally, without protagonists really understanding why this is possible. Solutions and successful events seem to be in line with more and more signs of new integration becoming visible. All this is experienced by internal staff, but is usually even more obvious to external observers. The partners reassure each other in their connectedness and co-operation expressing positive observations and intuitive expectations. Not all problems are solved yet, but many have somehow been "forgotten" without negative consequences. The sensation of crisis has faded.

9.3. Dilemma

9.3.1. What is a dilemma?

A dilemma is a problematic situation that either cannot be solved or not resolved within a given frame of reference. The solution patterns available to people in the dilemma do not lead to acceptable solutions. When they acknowledge being aware of them, they feel trapped. They may feel (mild or wild) despair without being able to pinpoint the situation they are in. This insolvability can be implausible from outside, because it is constituted mainly by internal ideas. There may be seemingly obvious solutions from an outside perspective, but the dilemma frame of reference does not allow them to be accepted. Therefore, it does not make sense to continue to invest in solutions within the dilemma system.

Still, it is not easy to prevent "insiders" from seeking such solutions which seem to protect them from painful insights.

Outside helpers then may feel despair instead, some with empathy, others with helplessness.

What can be done instead? First it is essential to identify one's own despair and openly deal with this perception without being able to pinpoint the logic of the problem or solutions. Neither is it easy to offer solidarity without knowing ways to escape, nor is it possible to acknowledge despair without being trapped oneself. Facing the shared present dilemma situation without losing self-confidence and power poses a challenge. Dealing competently with insights and feelings in dilemmas is crucial and has to be learned, especially with regard to the element of despair. With the dilemma model as a framework for joint investigations, the dilemma and insolvabilities may be identified. This helps people letting go of habitual patterns, and facing uncomfortable feelings and insights, thus developing trust.

Coping with dilemma may involve analyzing it on a content level on the one hand (9.3.2) and dealing with dilemma processes in experience and behavior on the other (9.3.3).

9.3.2. Logics of dilemma

From the point of outsider, one can analyze the dilemma framework without getting involved oneself. This can be done by hypothesizing dilemma equations, describing the dilemma framework. Each of these equations and their combination contribute to the insolvability of the dilemma e.g.

- *Questioning one's own quality of work, the strategy of managers and of staff, equals assuming mismanagement, thus losing respect and trust*

- *Taking time and resources for the restructuring the project, training of the employees, which need new qualifications equals opening up for an unacceptable delay and intolerable additional costs*

- *Doubting and even giving up a strategy once chosen equals outing as a procrastinator*

- *Empathetic leadership equals discussing everything with everyone*

- *Requiring increasing efforts equals oppressing people.*

Equations like these are usually not expressed explicitly, but they can be observed as behavior and discussed as hypotheses about internal frameworks deducted from experience. The question is whether people within dilemmas are available for reasoning. As long as people feel trapped, they are not easily available for discussing hypotheses on their reference frameworks. If they actually acknowledge these equations, they might become even more desperate. How can you invite getting in touch, still feeling desperate and uncomfortable insights which are part of the process? How can the partner be invited to consider external observation of their behavior and try hypotheses about underlying equations? Achieving this while keeping despair under control is difficult, as a dilemma usually goes along with denying insights that could lead to negative emotions.

To prepare dialogues, understanding the dilemma model as a possible tool for description is helpful. When explained in a general way accompanied by examples from others, people can more easily identify their own situation, catching their interest and motivation. Identifying one's own experience within the dilemma circle is a first step, followed more easily by the creation of hypotheses about dilemma equations.

External partners can describe their own experiences facing the dilemma situation with the partner without understanding the respective frames of reference behind. Thus, by starting with the dilemma circle, a dilemma frame of reference can be accessed more easily.

9.3.3. The dilemma circle

Dilemmas can be identified by experience cases in the dilemma circle. Dilemma dynamics arise from dilemma frameworks and at the same time these dynamics keep them valid and active.

Typical phases of dilemma experience are denial, struggling, exhaustion and despair:

Denial: As you are unaware of the dilemma, the situation seems to be unsuspicious. You downplay warning signals and act as if solutions were available. As long as there is no need for intensive engagement, the effects of the dilemma system are low.

Struggling: Efforts do not return the expected benefits, and trying harder turns into struggling at no end, i.e. making efforts, which are not carried by confidence. Once the lack of confidence has been identified, this may be a starting point for dilemma circle analysis.

Exhaustion: Sometimes struggling turns into exhaustion. To a certain extent exhaustion is a normal reaction after an endeavor to recover and to return with new energy and fresh ideas. The exhaustion of fighting a dilemma, however, differs in that it throws us back into the cycle. People tend to avoid identifying their hopelessness often deeming illness, drugs, or burnout as the only possible way to escape the situation.

Despair: Having struggled long enough, switching back and forth between struggling and exhaustion naturally leads to despair. Our culture can be described as phobic against despair, ignoring the notion that despair (mild or wild) clearly indicates an imbedded insolvability of a problem thus searching for an underlying dilemma. That is why it is a professional competence to deal with despair.

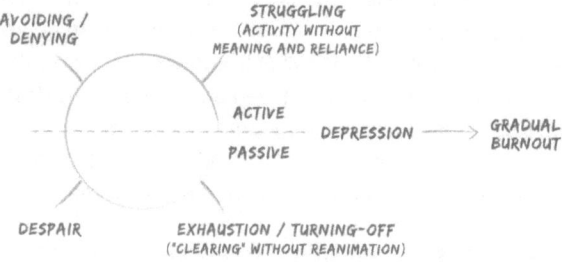

Fig. 30:   The dilemma circle (Schmid/Jäger 1986)

From a medical point of view, switching back and forth in the dilemma circle causes depression in its active and passive forms and in the long run to a so-called burnout.

9.3.4.   Helpful attitudes and approaches

Dealing with dilemmas is the premier service in a professional helping relationship.

Some recommendations for helping:

It is a real challenge to cope with people being caught in a dilemma circle and desperate. If you insist on indicating insolvability this may lead to the suspicion that you are the source of inconvenience. As a helper you may have already stepped into the dilemma circle yourself. Then the key is identifying your own situation. You may find you have been in the denial phase for some time already, and only now are you taking your experiences and observations seriously. You might want to focus on insolvability and dilemma behavior now, while your partners are stuck within the dilemma circle and refuse confrontation. Their additional dilemma is the fear of losing chances and a helping partnership when they acknowledge insolvability. Rather than being a nice caring person shielding off despair, you must be a confronting caring person who invites meeting despair and then guides through it, analyzing insolvability and raising hope for a meaningful reality beyond dilemma.

At this stage, it is key that you give up helping within the old frame of reference without blaming anyone, neither others nor yourself. What you need is a clear and impartial mind, as well as an awareness of denial, of your own despair, of dilemma struggles and exhaustion. You should be aware of the dilemma model, offer observations and have the courage of dialoguing. You need to learn to stay with your client, accepting your own helper's dilemma, but avoid sharing the client's dilemma. You need the courage to be temporarily present without solutions and explanations, not declaring this as incompetence. Avoid raising false hope, but rather be ready to bring despair to the surface, finding a position for yourself and support the acceptance of insolvability. Offer solidarity without the need to offer solutions. It's about accompanying feeling despair without going for changes prematurely.

For the helper there are also dilemmas during dissolving the dilemma before and afterwards. Be ready to recognize the situation changing without anybody realizing what you have done for it. This situation is a frequent follow-up dilemma. Often change happens without a plausible explanation, what the dilemma was and why it dissolved. It may be like waking up from a nightmare, which is fading before being understood sufficiently. This makes it hard to justify that your diagnosis and all the efforts have been necessary. The most important intervention may have been to face the dilemma, keeping up contact and dialogue.

9.3.5. Complexity and Dilemma

Missing complexity in solutions for complex problems may cause dilemmas.

Dilemmas can also be caused by not accepting obvious solutions to problems in time. Within the logic of dilemmas, undetected or not accepted insolvabilities may lead to more complexity. Illusionary expectations such as increasing complexity without a strategy for keeping up with resources and for developing an adequate organizational culture are problem boosters eventually turning into dilemmas.

Many companies drift into dilemmas, because they do not have a culture of in-time talking about the experience of feeling lost and desperate. Here a communication culture of trust generates existential opportunities. Talking about dilemma experience deliberately and identifying phases of dilemma circle paves the way of stopping to invest in old patterns and looking for real options. Thus, disintegration may be prevented and a crisis can be handled early without risking dramatic damages.

10. Sharing intuition and imagery

"A picture is worth a thousand words". I presume everybody experienced this.

I remember that once in an essay I was explaining why coaches should be competent in many ways, but the only point that was quoted by my colleagues was my dictum "coaches are decathletes". A complex discourse is condensed in one word, one sentence, an image, a short story, or one scene, which helps sharing the essential ideas. An image of a subject may convey its meaning or essence more effectively than a description ever could have. Narrative approaches do not really explain but elicit understanding in a holistic way. They provide a framework of understanding that can be filled and enriched with examples from the world of the recipient. They create internal realities connected with feelings and body sensations, which help to coordinate processes and to create memory beyond explainable categories. This is why narratives are so vital for both individuals and organizations.

10.1. The three swans

The isb uses the "three-swan metaphor" as an example to convey the idea of meta-perspectives on reality:

Tünnes and Schäl are two famous German comedy figures. Tünnes asks his friend Schäl to make a wish. Schäl wishes to be a swan, for the pleasure of being able to fly.

His friend Tünnes replies he' d rather be two swans – one to enjoy flying and one to consciously experience watching himself enjoying flying.

Inspired in turn Schäl decides to rather be three swans: Like Tünnes, he could be one to enjoy flying, one to consciously experience watching himself, and in addition, a third swan being able to watch the second swan who is watching the first swan, thus intensely enjoying the experience at all levels.

This metaphor can be used to create awareness of one's reality at different levels. However, we were intrigued by how many other distinctions can be used in three levels, usually conveying notions of "meta" and relationship between different levels of experiencing and analyzing.

10.2. What is intuition?

According to Aristotle, intuition is defined as "knowing" about reality, without knowing how we know. And usually we know little about what we know, but we act as if we knew. Thus, intuition stands for psyching out and for generating images of realities.

Intuition organizes realities, experiencing and acting. But intuition is neither natural nor mystical, it is based on learning and personal and cultural habits. These habits may include intuitive prejudice and repeated mistakes. There may be many fields of intuition untrained. This is why intuition can be either qualified or unqualified and may either guide or misguide. Intuition can lead towards reality and action either shared and functional or conflicting and dysfunctional. Qualifying intuition requires dialogues referring explicitly to intuitions and imagery building up a shared communication culture. This culture needs to integrate both conscious-methodical and unconscious-intuitive levels. (cf. chapter 1.5.)

- Professional intuition must be trained to become focussed according to which sphere is relevant and for which professional purposes it is required.

- Different professionals should have different masteries of intuition, as they deal with different spheres of reality, different roles, and different responsibilities.

10.3. What is imagery?

Imagery means referring to all kind of mental images of individuals or collectives. Imagery does not only deal with (visual) images, but includes all senses, all ways of perceiving and expressing reality beyond literal or explicit forms.

Imagery is about spontaneous ways in which people relate to themselves and to each other. Language is full of images, which we are often not aware of. Images create internal realities. People talk to themselves, both by relating to dreams or external experience and by daydreaming of all kind. People communicate by activating imageries reciprocally, using a narrative language and imbedding metaphors or referring to phantasies.

Communicating with the world of imagery and actively using imagery can be learned like any other complex language through guided practice and receiving some additional training in the underlying logics. Thus, everybody can learn to improve relating to imagery, and to use it to create and share intended realities.

Imagery usually happens affecting us spontaneously from behind the scenes. Training contributes to this, putting imagery in the foreground and purposely practicing the language related to it. As with other languages, once having learned to use it competently, it is drifting out of our awareness and operates with competence from the background.

Let me now describe some areas, through which we can practice the language of imagery.

10.4. Mental images and professional situations

Mental images are at work in the background of professional work and identity. They have an impact on which roles and scenarios we adopt, shape or experience as fateful and meaningful. In order to understand which roles, we tend to adopt and which stages and plays we are attracted to, we need to explore our own leading background images. By asking relatively simple questions, these inner background images, acting as energy fields and shaping professional performance and satisfaction can be identified.

Background images can help to examine 'matching' (cf. chapter 6.5) between your professional function in an organization and your personality. Do current and future requirements fit your personal motivations, values and skills? Background images in professional situations matter beyond the official criteria, also including the question of individuals' own essential elements of satisfaction.

One of the sources of images is remembering childhood imaginations. If as a child someone imagined becoming an engine driver, it makes a difference to which of the following inner pictures he or she is connected.

Here are three variations:

- „My engine and me – no one know it like I do!"

- „My stoker and me – two buddies travelling around the world!"

- „All passengers are relying on me. I'll get you there safe and sound".

Activating and comparing such inner images allow an intuitive grasp on meaning and matching. Developments in a team or organization illustrated by corresponding images may fit or may not fit the images for people's personal development. With the help of inner images, a dialogue of matching can be started which may contribute to the necessary clarification of whether an employee is ultimately able to develop full competence and satisfaction in a professional function and what kind of support is necessary. This is where criteria of professional personality development and organizational development meet.

10.5. Sharing intuition

A dialogue using inner images helps us get an impression of the developments of a team or a project. Do imaginations of future activities, roles and career have sufficient consistency? We assume that this matching of intuitive imaginations of people involved is of decisive importance for self-motivation and self-control, for creative potentials and their interplay. The less the projects can be planned and leaders can keep an eye on all essentials, the more this is valid. In complex situations the processes of co-ordination are so challenging that it evades conscious control, shifting the need for co-ordination to intuitive control. Working with inner images enhances contact with oneself and one's inner strengths. At the same time, it strengthens the intuitive, creative interplay between those joining a force field.

Activating inner images and metaphorical communication leads to more effective intuition as it becomes an integral part of professional communication culture in a company.

10.6. Guided imagery

Guided imagery can help to become aware of stories influencing us from background and promote narrative dialoguing. Guided imagery links many approaches and labels, e.g. guided daydreams, trance, or relaxation techniques. The basic scheme starts by inviting people to relax and reduce their orientation to the outside, opening them up to internal processes and images. Then some content may be focused through the facilitator. For example, background images of a particular current experience of situations may be focused. Then people are invited to translate these images into the present and to be become aware of how they relate to presence. Dialogue with others about such experiences can activate mutual understanding and increase resonance of others. Thus, multi-layered and deeper feedback and sharing further ideas comes into play. Dialogue on imagery can bring core insights to the understanding of personal development.

Note this example:

After a guided imagery on background images of one's professional career, a senior executive coach shared his childhood memories of which he had not been aware of for at least 30 years: *"We lived in a small town, where my father was the only doctor. One day, the owner of the major factory in that town went crazy and ran around the town naked. He was a prominent person, and nobody had any idea what to do, so they called my father for help. He did it. He came home and told the family of his personal satisfaction that he had somehow managed to keep the guy from behaving madly without one of them losing his face.*

At this own insight, he burst out saying "Oh my God. I have done this all my professional life!"

10.7. Stories and rituals

As in the above example, stories can be triggered spontaneously when reflecting individual frames of references in the background of individuals. However, stories can also reflect the perception of an organization, its history and culture. Although they may not be "real" in many respects, they give a subjective orientation about qualities and expectations associated with them. This is why a dialogue on such stories and how they are affecting people in the organization may be relevant.

Look at this example:

There was great resistance against the restructuring of a metallurgic company due to technical developments. In search of stories related to the problem at that time, many stories were told about how the company's restructuring two decades before had traumatized the families of the employees. By this time, the younger family members in the new buildings had been idealized, while the generation of fathers and uncles, who had spent their whole lives developing the company, was neglected in the old buildings in a degrading manner. As this experience had influenced family life at home, but had found no place in organizational communication, the responses to the restructuring plans at the time were negative and diffuse. After all this was discussed, the installation of rituals of appreciation for the degraded generation reconciled the employees with the past and prepared the ground for rebuilding of the company.

10.8. Dreams

Dreams can be interpreted as "acts of visualizing and commenting on important issues and challenges in personal and professional life".

Working on and with dreams can serve

1. To better comprehend experience in professional situations, i.e. retrospectively understand what has touched, prospectively grasp what is yet to come.

2. To provoke new and alternative perspectives on old problems and to correct restrictive expectations.

3. To correct and supplement existing patterns and styles (cf. chapter 11).

4. To reflect and comment on professional development from a psychological perspective.

5. To activate storytelling using dreams as a means of expression.

Dealing with dreams provides the opportunity to practice symbolic understanding and to work with symbolic material. Creative work with dream narratives can help us master the interplay between conscious-methodical and unconscious-intuitive work.

Careful exchange in a suitable professional group can help to secure the intuition for work and personal development.

Dreams tell stories either tragic or funny, realistic or surrealistic, lyrical or prosaic, dramatic or grotesque. Telling dreams is usually motivated by the desire to discover their meaning, especially when intensive emotions are involved. Dialogues about dreams can inspire new ideas, patterns, and styles as creative alternatives to the story they tell. Note that dreams never represent reality as such. They create their own "dream realities", which are developed with narrative means.

In an organizational context, psychotherapeutic approaches to dreams are inappropriate, and normally no dream experts are at work. However, dialogue about dreams can open up to understand what is happening on the backstage and resonate with it. Dialogue about dreams, e.g. in a project team, can encourage to disclose mutually intuitive relationships and to communicate subjective developments. This can be done by anyone, i.e. it does not require expert status. Being creative and experimental is a universal talent. But some methodical instructions can be helpful. Whether it contributes to the enrichment of the organization depends on the culture of communication and relationships in general.

10.9. The theatre metaphor

To understand and talk about how reality is created, theatre is a perfect image of life to be studied. On stage, reality is deliberately enacted and everyone knows many components to create that reality. Therefore, most people are intuitively able to use metaphors from the theatre in a simple way, making the components of creating a play a perfect setting for directly discussing the genius of reality.

For contexts that consider both personal work and organizational reality, we start with five key components, i.e. roles, stages, themes, stories, and styles of play.

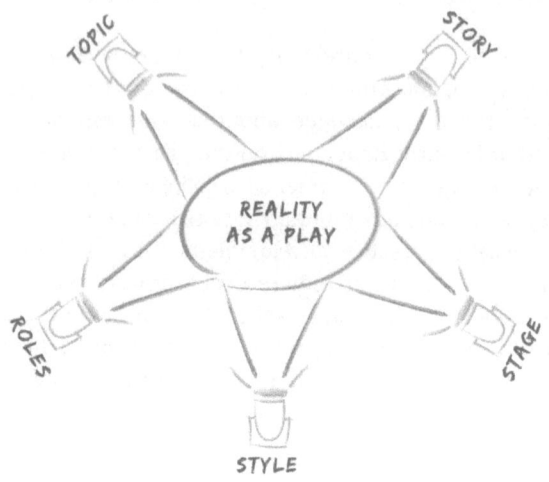

Fig. 31: Reality illustrated by the theatre -metaphor (Schmid/Wengel 2001)

Supposing Shakespeare's "King Lear" is performed, and we find, for example, the role of the king, the roles of the "un-faithful" daughters and of the "faithful" one, the role of the faithful servant, etc.

The play deals with topics such as trust, naivety, greed for power, "black" ingratitude, betrayal and cruelty. The story tells that a powerful man who is tired of being king wants to give up his power and change his life in order to be loved and given generosity and gratitude. But he is naive and misjudges the character of both the situation and his own children. Thus, he opens the stage of betrayal and loses everything. Both his family and his kingdom are in tragic self-destruction. Which stages can this play be performed on?

It can be performed on big stages with many players as well as on small stages. Scenes can be played open on main stages or hidden in rooms behind the official stage. Thus, the style of the play can either be opulent to celebrate the orchestration of royal attributes and battles, or it can be reduced to the key players in outfits and styles like you and me. It can be played with intensive expressions of feeling or by only expressing only the essentials low-voiced or non-verbal.

In the theatre there are other components and functions such as "Who is writing the script?", and "Who is directing the play?". However, we usually start by asking, "What are the topics and in what story are they treated?", "In which scenes is the story enrolled?", "What roles are there and what are the relationships?", "On which stages is the play performed in which style?"

10.10. Personality represented by theatre metaphor

The "theatre metaphor" can be used for an illustrative description of personality (see Fig. 32). However, the description does not relate primarily to a psychological or a biographical understanding of a personality, but to how someone metaphorically performs his or her personality in life episodes. Questions of personality are therefore concrete within in a temporal and local framework. Without particular expertise, everyone can contribute and comment on his or her observations, intuitions, and fantasies. While not plausible, it is interesting to know about them, as they usually affect others' attitudes and behavior anyway.

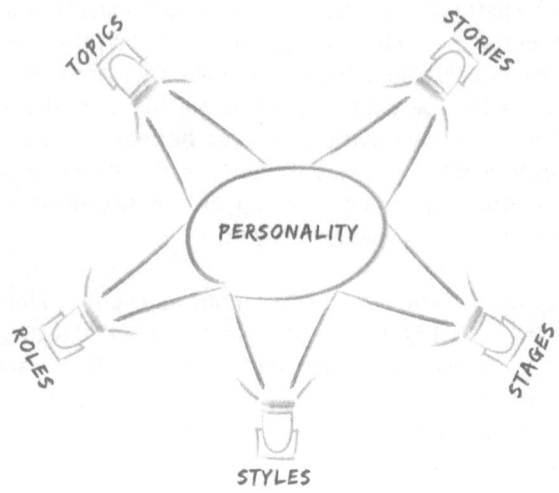

Fig. 32:   Personality illustrated by the theatre metaphor
(Schmid/Wengel 2001)

Each personality can be described as a portfolio of roles, themes, stages, and plays as well as styles, in which things are expressed. These components include the entire personality in action. By carefully examining the portfolio, we can identify the actual personality, but also gain intuitive insight into the personality traits that remain in the background, the hidden personality. Together the sequence of life scenes and their qualities reflect the life's course (curriculum vitae) and its meaning.

When thinking about change, it makes a difference whether the combination of a person's roles, topics, stories, stages, or styles gives a chance to succeed.

Normally, it is not difficult to get good hints from others. For example, someone actually learns that not the change of topics or roles, but rather changing stages or styles would help to develop better plays.

10.11. Organization and theatre metaphor

The culture of an organization corresponds to the personality of an individual. The structure of time, performance, and satisfaction are not only perspectives for individuals, but also for organizations. Based on the theatre metaphor, the culture of an organization can be identified and particular relationships within teams, organizations and departments can be look at.

As long as a team and organizational culture are quite homogenous, reality seems "natural" and not like enacted reality. But when different ways of shaping reality meet in new teams or new reality should be realized, it is much more plausible, that reality is to be created and it needs to be discussed how to design and implement it. This is all the truer of mergers where very different cultures can clash. Often the protagonists in such processes underestimate the efforts needed to share different views and habits and to find ways to integrate realities and ways to implement them. It is no surprise that so many mergers fail, even if this is economically feasible.

Here the theatre metaphor can help to discuss views with the theater metaphor. (see Fig. 33) After all, this is not only a contribution to make mergers more successful and more satisfying, but also an opportunity to reflect and promote ways to create reality on all sides.

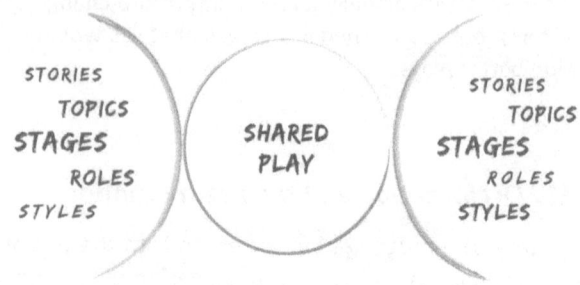

Fig. 33: Relationships illustrated by the theatre metaphor
(Schmid/Wengel 2001)

11. Sharing reality styles

11.1. Why styles?

Whether life sharing and creating reality is enriching depends on the matching of styles in more situations than we are normally aware of. Apart from WHAT others play on shared stages, we are usually heavily influenced by HOW they play. Donald Trump or Angela Merkel have very different styles, regardless of what they do on the content level or what role they play. A strategic meeting in a military unit is different from a Greenpeace meeting, no matter what the topic is.

Professional style resembles a kind of dancing. Similar to the culture and dance practice, it is always about practicing again and again. Learning of a style cannot be achieved by learning a single dance. It is understood over time by training the intended style in different dance sections until it achieves one embodiment. Then the style can be transferred to dances, even those that have never been practiced. Everyone can immediately feel that there is a match with the intended style, even without being able to name the indicators for that assessment.

Let us try defining the style: "Style" is a "container term" that generally describes how people and systems organize and express themselves. For example, how do people relate to tension, and relaxation when they interact? Some become quieter and more concentrated others louder and more agitated.

Style descriptions can be used for individuals and for groups. But they can also be used to describe the culture of larger configurations such as teams, departments, and organizations. Interestingly, we find style traditions that persist, although currently no promoters can be identified.

As in other cultural dimensions, style seems to be an area in which it is usually reproduced unconsciously. To investigate how styles survive and adapt and how they can be selectively changed (cf. chapter 7.7 Systems learning) can be an eye-opener.

Satisfaction in professional and personal relationships depends to a large extent on the consistency of styles, whether you have a positive attitude to other styles or are allergic to them. Failure to clarify styles can lead to dissatisfaction and loss of strength. Mismatches in styles are often understood as disagreements in other areas. Dialogue on styles as an accepted part of communication can help maintain connectivity and performance. This can prevent irritation in the early phases of relationships and open the way for clarification. However, this type of meta-communication requires a language suitable for the discussion of styles, and therefore requires experience in dialogue with other styles.

Later in this chapter you will find an overview of some concepts for styles, which have proven themselves in the professional field. (11.7-11.15).

11.2. Dialoging on styles

Everyone responds to styles. Decisions are made in many relationships and processes more or less consciously for style reasons. Normally, the influence of styles remains unconscious or is deliberately hidden. If you become aware of the styles, this can lead to targeted discussions to enable more appropriate versions and possibly further developed styles. In our culture, it is quite unusual to talk explicitly about styles because style is experienced as something natural, personal, and intimate as the human body. Overcoming this taboo opens the door to active dialogues about styles and mutual learning.

Let us look at this example:

Once a year I visit our training groups and do some coaching illustrating our style. Instead of having a general warm-up conversation and then starting coaching, I decide to first talk to the coachees and the training group about our personal styles. In order to reach an eye-level relationship, I tell them that they have known themselves for many years. We all are experts of our own experience and can tell others what works with us and how. That is why we need to exchange some instructions about stile. The motto is: "What you should know about me considering the way I am constructed. or "If you want to have an enriching and pleasant encounter with me, here are my user instructions." Then we check if our expectations match. We also arrange for the meta-communication session to be interrupted whenever necessary. I also give instructions about my approach and stile of work.

Instructions about ones Style (Example)

1. I work intuitively. If something comes to my mind, I offer it as research material. It may turn out to be relevant or not. If not, I abandon it.

2. If I have an observation concerning the process, I`ll mention it, if you agree. There is no need to deal with it immediately. It is meant to be saved just in case you want to look at it later.

3. I do not limit my comments to what can be dealt with in the situation, but rather comment on what seems interesting. It is audio-recorded so you can later listen to it and discuss it with colleagues.

4. Please let me know if you find any of my behavior irritating. I am quite tolerant and you can talk openly with me, just as you feel and think.

5. I often do not dig deeper because patterns on the surface seem more important. I often prefer to experiment with new perspectives in order to take a closer look at what we have already seen.

6. I tend to take things lightly when appropriate. Life is heavy enough to make it as comfortable as possible with humor.

7. I work transparently. If you want to better understand what I mean, just ask and I will tell you.

8. Let's be a study group. If I "chew" on an idea but do not grab it right away, I will tell you. It might be relevant. So, let us co-operate to find out and sharpen, what is important.

9. I tend to sit with arms crossed. Please do not take this as defensive attitude against you. Choose the degree of eye-contact and of the expression of the emotions the way you feel comfortable. I am ready to handle your emotions, but leave it up to you to decide to what degree you want to get into it.

10. I give you instruction or advice, whenever I find it useful. If you feel it is inappropriate or not helpful, just let me know.

Self-declarations and offers like these illustrate my personal style and context. Apart from the fact that it provokes useful conversations on self-control and responsibility it is an interesting self-experience to formulate such self-descriptions and receive feedback on them and whether my following behavior is congruent. In teams or work groups, different types of statements may be appropriate.

11.3. Self-discovery on styles

Since most people are unaware of the styles and not used to talking about them, they need self-awareness that is facilitated by exercises and questions focusing on styles. Exercises of self-discovery of styles can bring people into contact with their current style and its history.

Questions for Self-discovery around styles:

1. Someone else is dealing a situation in a surprisingly different way than you would have done. Give an example. How would you describe the differences?

2. Imagine an event where you spontaneously feel "at home" and you have the feeling "This is exactly the way things should be handled". How would you describe this experience and its components?

3. How would you describe the person with whom you easily resonate? What tends to irritate you in relationships? What do your descriptions tell about what style matters to you?

4. Suppose you discuss an important professional issue with trusted colleagues. What is the style in which this particular group deals with it?

5. Suppose the same issues were discussed in an official meeting or in presence of bosses. How would that change?

6. What comments concerning from your spouse / friends / colleagues do you remember, when they wanted to describe "typical you"?

7. Which anecdotes or episodes people would tell if they wanted to illustrate 'This was once more typically you!'?

8. In what environment did you grow up? Which were typical ways of dealing with problems and people there? How did you feel about it?

9. When you look at situations in both your private and professional world, what are the similarities and where do they differ?

10. In which situations do you have intensive influence on others? How do you do it? What kind of atmosphere do you create?

11. When do you experience that the style of a team (a department, a company) is different from your personal style? What exactly are the differences? What are the advantages and disadvantages of these differences?

12. When you experience an encounter of two teams / departments / organizations which deal with issues of common interest, which differences in style can you identify? How do you explain these differences?

11.4. Feedback and Mirroring

When exploring the specifics of your style, you need feedback and mirroring from others.

Feedback should usually provide more operational information avoid just labeling (like "disinterested") but describe empiric observations of behavior (not looking at speaker, disrupt and talk about something else without any connection) and its elicited reactions (partner looks irritated and lost, withdraws or begins to act angry). Feedback should be more characterizing than valuing. Learning how to specifically describe elements of behavior prevents from acting on uncontrolled phantasies and projections. Combined for example with the role model, feedback also provides an exchange about role adequate behavior. It is usually helpful to receive a variety of feedback from different partners. Thus, weighting of observations and identifying of significant pattern gets a better chance.

The term mirroring is usually used, when more intuitive impressions are included and images and narratives are used for descriptions. Instead of step by step impact of behavior complex impressions and resonance is in the focus. "When I see you interacting, I cannot feel whether and how you are interested, in what this person tries to say. I miss a supporting attitude and I imagine, that I would not feel like sharing sensible things with you. This is why I would rather avoid serious conversation or even not wanting to listen in a sensible way, when it is your turn to speak.

When I say this I realize, that this happened several times without my awareness and I feel urged to change our contact into an enriching encounter!"

Being mirrored by others, receiving and understanding resonance on one's way of being, behaving and our style is a basic desire of humans. Building up a communication culture in which these needs are met in a qualified and for the context adequate way is a powerful contribution to organizational culture. Mirroring combined with intuitive and narrative approaches as described in Chapt. 10 is even more powerful and creates a lot of relatedness. This is why investing into feedback and mirroring and really becoming good is worth it.

11.5. Milieus and Styles

There is no free choice of developing styles for an individual or an organization. Styles always have a history and are determined by the milieus in which the individual has grown up or the organization has developed. Whenever individuals or organizations meet, it is their milieus that meet as well.

Especially middle-class people tend to deny this influence. This might have to do with them not wanting to deal with irritations for example anxiety of losing status or of not keeping up with others who appear to be better equipped. They aspire to either become a member of or at least be considered important for privileged milieus. Members of privileged milieus have an immediate and sensible awareness as to whether others share their milieu or do not. They will certainly neither lay open the consequences this entails nor be interested in discussing their privileges and have "envy-debates" about them.

This is particularly true, if they hope that "milieu-crossing relationships" have benefits for them.

However, professionals should be aware of milieu barriers, otherwise they may not understand, why they fail to gain certain positions or influence. Aspiring middle-class professionals, for example, are dedicated to performance and may not understand that for upper-class people performance is less important than status and networking. To be aware of milieu influence is also important for the factors energy and dignity. As discussed in chapters 6.3 and 6.4, it is possible to develop an appropriate level of both role competence and context competence. But then it is a separate question whether this really comes from a heart possibly still bound and loyal to the milieus one comes from. Even if one succeeds in becoming an accepted member of desired milieus, it may be at the expense of a lot of energy, or one might not feel at home on one's career path. There are no predefined answers to questions like these, but it is important to give such considerations a chance by taking them into account. It was Confucius who said, "It is a question of maturity and dignity identifying your place in life and accepting it." This is certainly not an argument not to look for choices of milieu.

11.6. Identity beliefs

"Who am I?" is a question moving human beings throughout their lives. People look for an identity, always in search of a self-definition they find appropriate. They are trying to avoid adopting such self-definitions that are not appropriate or even restrictive or self-destructive. This is why young boys identify with superman but hate others calling them "cowards".

Nevertheless, you may under specific circumstances accept an identity attribution like coward, even though you hate it. Having accepted an identity attribution, this remains in the background. Even successful trials of acting brave, doesn't change the belief, to be a coward. If you behave like a coward according the belief or still see yourself as a coward, who acts bravely, the identity belief doesn't change. We do not know much about the conditions leading to change of identity beliefs. However, this happens in most cases during human interaction through a kind of mirroring.

Sometimes people are caught in an adopted inappropriate identity belief, either behaving in accordance with it or struggling against it. Both feels wrong, as the underlying identity belief is not corrected. Interestingly enough, others intuitively identify such a belief behind the according behavior or the rebellion against, which points to it. Then they tune into the system by not questioning the belief, but reassure it by joining the assumption with or without awareness.

As with dilemmas (cf. chapter 9.3) it is important to know the concept of identity beliefs to be able really to help people caught in the situation. You need to focus on identity beliefs as false, although behavior makes the wrong belief plausible and seemingly authentic. It is important to know, that neither intended behavior nor experience alone change identity beliefs. An extra "mechanism" is needed to carry any change through to the identity-belief level.

This may be the ritual: "Changing identity card"

Let us look at a brief example on how a professional identity belief was changed.

A psychotherapist having had several years of education and practice as an organizational consultant came to a coaching session, complaining that whenever discussing with a CEO, he feels like losing all power and all orientation, even around questions dealt with several times before. This might have to do with his father who never believed he could be a successful organizational consultant and his former professional mentor did not like his plan to now change into that business. Inside, he still feels like being a psychotherapist playing an organizational consultant. He then either somehow withdraws acting like a psychotherapist or rebels by talking extremely like a businessman. Neither performance convinces himself let alone the CEO.

Therefore, in a ritual I asked him about his virtual identity card and said, "I am an authority both in the field of psychotherapy and in the field of Organizational Consulting. Looking at the identity card I see, "psychotherapist" written as an unchangeable attribute. To complete according to what is reality nowadays, I insert "Organizational Consultant" and sign it officially. Now your identity as an Organizational Consultant is truly and officially declared no matter whether you behave like the one. You cannot and do not have to prove anything through your behavior." "You do not even have to believe it yourself. Because it is in the document, it is nevertheless true."

This paradox message changed somehow the underlying identity restriction. From that moment onwards, not only did the described difficulties disappear, but he felt like an organizational consultant without paying much attention to the issue. And he stopped taking further training, because it was not necessary. Unspectacular but essential changes in identity beliefs may lead to dramatic manifestations of change.

11.7. Personality and isb approved style concepts

Frequently in professional training groups concepts taken from personality psychology and psychotherapy are used to describe personality and individual styles.

But usually those concepts cannot be rolled out for learning within organizations, as they are not accepted in a non-psychological field. As isb-participants are professionals with all kind of backgrounds, it is important to use a language and approaches, which can easily be understood and in a self-directed mode be applied within their own fields. This determines the following choice of useful concepts which have been developed or adapted at the isb for more general use beyond psychology.

11.8. I-IT and I-YOU-Style

I - IT-style people prefer to focus on content, purpose and performance. Their preferred focus in relationships is topics and achieving an outcome. They relate well in relationships as long as their preference is matched.

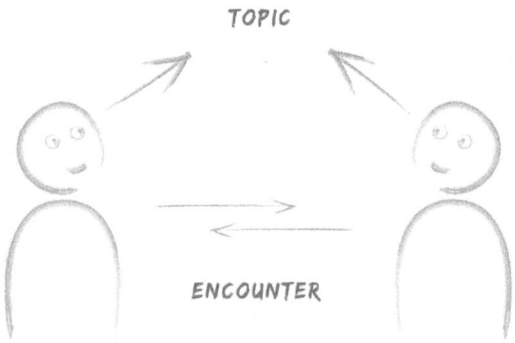

Fig. 34:   I <–> IT Preference Type (SCHMID 1998)

I –YOU-style people are oriented towards other people, relatedness and mutual respect. They take an interest in topics and perform well if they feel valued in a relationship and respected as individuals. I-YOU people are motivated to achieve goals, as long as they feel good in relationships.

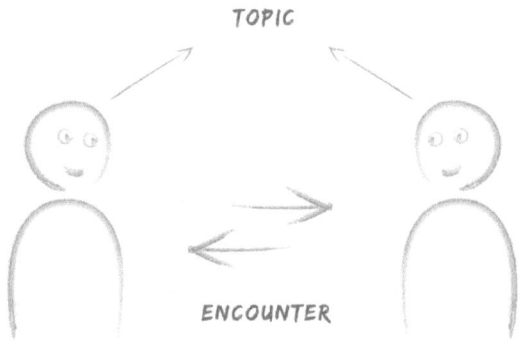

Fig. 35:   I <–> YOU Preference Type (SCHMID 1998)

These different relationship styles determine communication a lot. If there is a conflict and mutual polarization, style differences may appear extreme and incompatible. Then the I-IT-style calls for first fixing the shared interest in topics and purposes, whereas an I-You-style calls for first fixing mutual understanding and respect. Frequently these two positions become polarized turning against each other. In order to move to an area of compatibility, each should first be motivated to honor the other style. Once both styles become more complementary again, conflicts on topics and power often disappear.

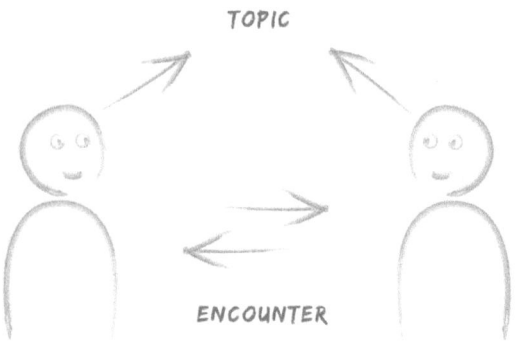

Fig. 36:   Integrate I <–> YOU / I <–> IT Type (SCHMID 1998)

Although different styles can be balanced under normal conditions, differences may again pop up and polarize under pressure, making balancing and integrating even more important. Sometimes the style of a group or organization becomes too one-sided I-YOU or I-IT.

Once people understand their own style and are willing to understand styles of others, they gain the ability to choose and adopt their communication patterns appropriately matching both styles. When people learn to communicate on different styles and on how to get along with the difference, they can de-escalate conflicts and learn to negotiate shared styles. Everyone should learn to value both dimensions and how to make contact in respect to others' preferences, especially in conflicts.

11.9. Exercise I-YOU / I - IT Style

Consciously dealing with the opposite style makes leadership and co-operation more successful and satisfying.

Consider this exercise: Think of a person in your organization, you have difficulties to influence and communicate with. Ask yourself, "What is my relationship-style "I-IT or I-YOU"? "What do I think is the style of the other person? If you were to try and meet this person's style, what would be different? How would you feel? What would you hope and fear? Do you know somebody, who is getting along with this person well? Why? What makes the difference?

If you develop attention along the questions above, it will help you navigate your perception and communication. If you fail to understand another person's style, it feels like knocking the wrong door.

11.10. Excitement intensifier and reducer

There are two styles of expression around excitement we call "excitement intensifiers" and "excitement reducers". Any organization will have a mixture of both styles or types.

People who are excitement intensifiers welcome excitement, as it is their way to express that they experience or search for something essential. Excitement reducers do not really welcome excitement. Being calm is their way of expressing themselves when they experience or seek something essential.

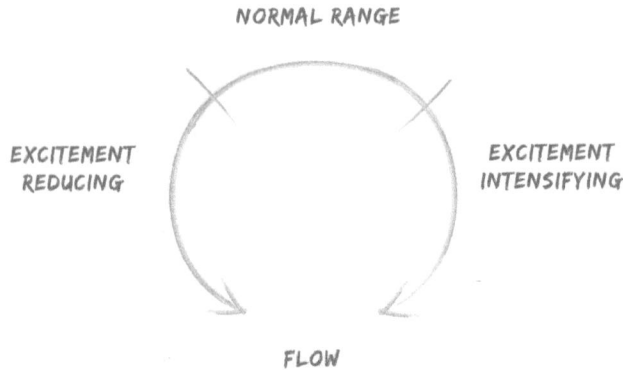

NORMAL RANGE

EXCITEMENT
REDUCING

EXCITEMENT
INTENSIFYING

FLOW

Fig. 37: Handling Excitement (Schmid 1998)

Excitement intensifiers prefer issues and relationships which giving them opportunities to be exited and express their feelings. They are irritated by silence and need things to get heated up to feel comfortable. Excitement reducers may take up an idea and work on it, but may still not show excitement or express their feelings. They are irritated by intensity and need things to cool down to feel comfortable. Both styles should be accepted corresponding to two types of meditating, e.g. Sufi dancing vs. sitting in ZEN-Meditation. However, the combination obviously appears as difficult. The conflict arises as one expects the opposite participant to respond in the own way.

We frequently observe excitement intensifiers trying to persuade the excitement reducers to share their excitement about their ideas. Such persuasion attempts tend to achieve the contrary. The excitement reducers may feel stressed wondering why the other person is so overwhelming or ungrounded. Similarly, when the reducer asks people to calm down, this can be stressful for excitement intensifiers. Either can become addicted to their own style, sticking to it habitually, unaware that they would approach something more essential if they were to move in direction of the other style. Therefor an organization needs to make the best of both styles dialoguing on which combinations are helpful in which situations. Understanding this concept of excitement intensifier and excitement reducers will help understand the differences of each side expressing themselves and help avoiding conflicts arising at work.

11.11. Extraversion versus Introversion

C.G. Jung (1921) defined "extraversion" as "attention and energy of a human being tending to face outwards", and "introversion" as "predominantly tending to face inwards". Since Jung's days, the concept of "Extraversion versus Introversion" has reached high popularity being used in a variety of areas.

Being more extraverted or more introverted always has grace and burden depending on the predominant orientation of the context.

Even if one can flexibly adapt to a more outward or inward orientation depending on role, activity and context, it is important to be aware of what prevails. This can help understand both the past social and emotional developments as well as the current situation.

"Extraversion versus Introversion" is not a homogeneous concept, but rather a combination of various components. Let us outline four components, which are combined with four corresponding scales from 1 to 7. Adding the scale numbers of all four scales indicates an overall orientation.

11.11.1. Attention

My attention is more often directed on my inner self and to myself. Being aware of others and what happens outside myself sometimes falls short. ← → My attention is more often directed to the outside and to others. Being aware of myself and of what happens inside me sometimes falls short.

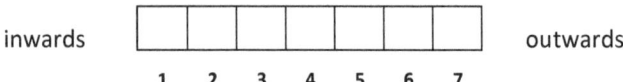

inwards   1   2   3   4   5   6   7   outwards

11.11.2. Social flexibility

When I encounter strangers and informal situations without having a specific function, I feel self-conscious ← → completely not self-conscious.

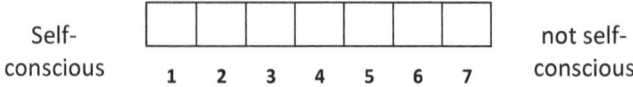

Self-conscious   1   2   3   4   5   6   7   not self-conscious

11.11.3. Energy balance

Being on public stages and in more official contact exhausts my batteries and I need recharging ← → The public stage is exactly what charges my batteries making me feel energized.

batteries exhausting								batteries charging

1   2   3   4   5   6   7

11.11.4. <u>Being oneself</u>

Whenever I feel I am losing contact to myself, I withdraw into familiar surroundings and focus on my topics. ← → I like to go „on tour", adding inspirations with new encounters.

Self-centering in familiar surroundings

1   2   3   4   5   6   7

Adding inspirations with new encounters

For a total score please add the four numbers for attention, social flexibility, energy balance and being oneself:

163

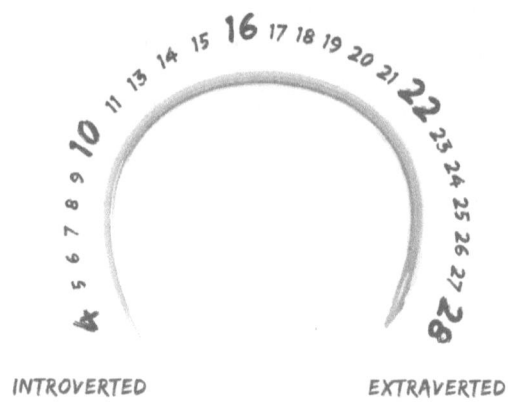

INTROVERTED   EXTRAVERTED

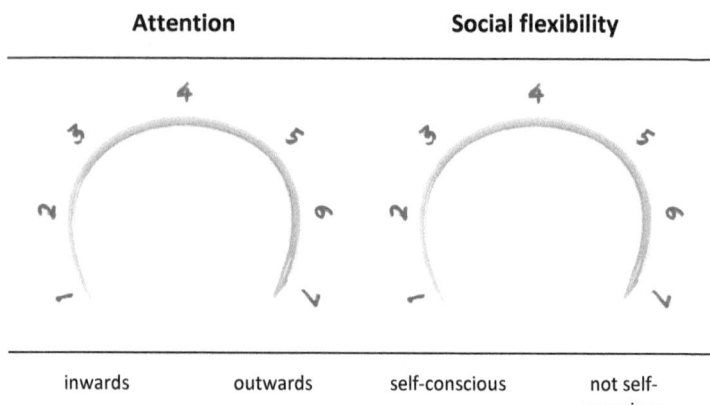

Attention		Social flexibility	
inwards	outwards	self-conscious	not self-conscious

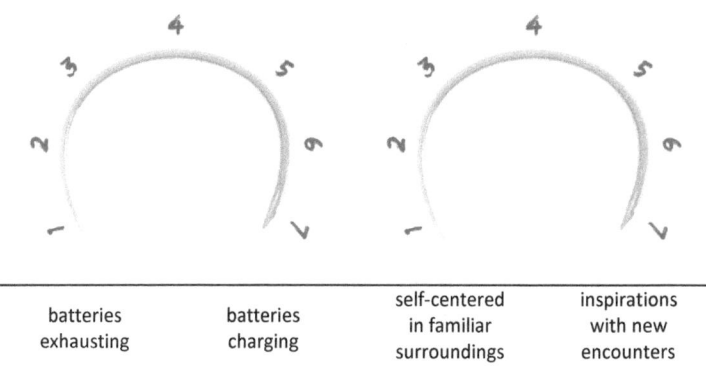

Energy balance		Being oneself	
batteries exhausting	batteries charging	self-centered in familiar surroundings	inspirations with new encounters

Fig. 38: Extraversion and introversion

11.12. Approach and avoidance styles

In unclear situations, "approaching people" tend to diminish distance and "avoiding people" tend to increase distance. Expressions e.g. "I want to, let's get into it, let's just do it, just go ahead" all characterize approach-style people. Expressions like "I don't really want to, what will happen if?", "Did we consider all potential pitfalls before getting into action?" best describe avoidance-style people. People who tend to organize themselves by avoiding things can easily be "branded" as people with negative thoughts or as persons of retreat. However, let us acknowledge the strength of avoidance-based thinkers.

They give priority to "safety first" or Reflecting first" tending not to surrender beyond what they can be held responsible for. Once they feel safe and secure, these people usually show that they are prepared to come out of their shell.

Avoidance by staying distant may be an escape from contact. On the other hand, the nature of the approach-style can also be an escape from being in contact by fleeing to the front "taking the bull by the horns". Their strengths are being dynamic, approaching actions and judgments, doing something, rather than just considering and talking. This may give them the necessary drive to get things done and involve others.

Putting it in a metaphor, if you drive your car into a muddy area, you may need speed to get through. If you stop or slow down in the middle, you will probably get stuck. If you drive on ice and speed up too much, the situation may get out of control or you will 'spin the wheel' not getting anywhere. You should rather stop, prepare the situation (e.g. by using sand) and then slowly try to move again.

Therefore, you need to have both styles available in order to have the ability to assess the situation you are in. Since this is often unclear, you need to experiment with both styles and see what will work.

11.13. Detail and the big picture

Some people tend to think in detail and some think in more general terms. The person who prefers the "big picture" may express himself in terms of "this project will work", but this may not appeal to the person who prefers "details". The latter would like to know exactly how this project will work and the criteria that will ensure that this project works. Such "details thinking" will help to capture the reality of the context.

The common bias against the "detail thinker" is that they may get lost in detail. They cannot see the forest in front of the trees.

The "big picture thinker" has the strength to create a wider picture using a general frame, but may lose the details. They see the forest losing sight of the trees. What we eventually need is a balance between the overall picture and the details.

"Big picture people" can learn to break big ideas into examples that illustrate them. This is exactly what "details people" need to believe that the big picture is valid and worth developing. Daily learning for the "big picture" people is when you can provide examples on demand. This gives them an opportunity to establish contact with "detail people", but also to clarify how the big picture can be realized in real life.

"Details people" are at risk of losing orientation while accumulating details. Their ideas and contributions to a larger picture take the form of a series of detailed descriptions having to get abstracted as ideas. Their daily learning is the answer to the question "What is your description an example of?".

11.14. Evaluation of contributions

Although we all want to contribute, we have no shared yardstick against which to measure contributions. Everyone wants his/her contributions to be seen and acknowledged. Sometimes, others do not recognize or appreciate contributions, which I count in my balance between give and take. Whenever I do not feel accepted in my giving, I get into some kind of accounting emergency (Helm Stierlin). Something I want to be recognized for by others is simply not considered value to our joint accomplishment. The reason may be that they do not value what I claim for my account as my contribution to our shared give-and-take. Perhaps they really have other requirements for what would be of value for them and the company. As we all use different criteria for the assessment of contributions, all stakeholders should clarify what their specific contributions are and synchronize them with those responsible for accounting. The way they look at it and whether they are willing to accept these relationship values determines the common balance of give and take. This is not intended to mean that all contributions should be converted into trading values, limiting all experience and behavior to this reference framework. However, disappointments and the struggle for the respect that someone expects are often the result of not jointly clarifying to what extent the offered contributions have been mutually accepted. This makes dialogues illustrating a common understanding of contributions an essential part of sharing realities.

11.15. Typology by C. G. Jung

The psychiatrist Carl Gustav Jung created a model called "typology" indicating different ways people refer to reality.

Jung defines four ways of access to reality as independent and complementary so that we have different approaches to reality that never replace each other. All access has to be developed and only by meaningful completion do they form a complete picture of the reference to realities. Here is a brief description of his model. Jung postulates there are two direct accesses to reality i.e. the perceiving of existing reality and the visioning of possible realities.

Realities in organizations created and sustained by human interaction evoke perceptions, i.e. indications perceivable by the senses. This is one half of the reality experienced, though many people believe that this is the whole picture. We may call it sense for reality. The vision, which could also be considered as possible reality, is sufficient for the other half of the picture. This reality is potential, but has not yet been realized as such. Jung assumes that there are realities that have the potential to become a present reality rather than other theoretical possibilities for realities. The psychological function that captures this sense for potential can be called visioning.

Many orientations in management or consulting are related to a "flair for the possible" without providing a corresponding concept. A potential reality can be completely different from the current one and could now be produced or born to replace it.

Perceiving and visioning are direct accesses to reality. Furthermore, Jung postulates two ways of processing the impressions gained through the sense for reality and potentiality. These are Thinking and Evaluating. Thinking, on the one hand, involves establishing an intellectual order for the data obtained, and, on the other hand, evaluating means weighting reality not according to its content but according to its value to distinguish between the meaningful and the meaningless. Evaluating is the psychic function that assigns meaning to reality or sometimes detects a loss of meaning despite accuracy. For this education around values and something like an inner voice is of importance. More content doesn't replace meaning and feeling value doesn't replace clarification on a content level.

Only combining both allows sound judgments and is more efficient preventing efforts in wrong modus.

In all four functions orientation and variety have to be developed equally in diverse processes of learning. Perceiving and

Thinking can be learned "objectively" for example through media. This access to reality is the domain of science. But obviously people also relate to spheres, which can't be explained in this way. Such accesses to reality called Visioning and Evaluating here, are often mistaken as to be spontaneous and do not have to be qualified by learning. In fact, these are mostly habits, good or bad, gained through unconscious learning that can and should be improved through learning. But Evaluating and Visioning cannot be learned through explanations alone. It is about understanding. Learning within human relationships and resonance from those who are further developed in these areas, is needed.

Based on his vast experience, C.G. Jung quite plausibly argues that everyone initially develops two functions in the schematic representation side by side (see fig. 39), whereby the access to the reality has priority and the draft horses metaphorically stand for a long time in the quadruple of its interpretation of reality.

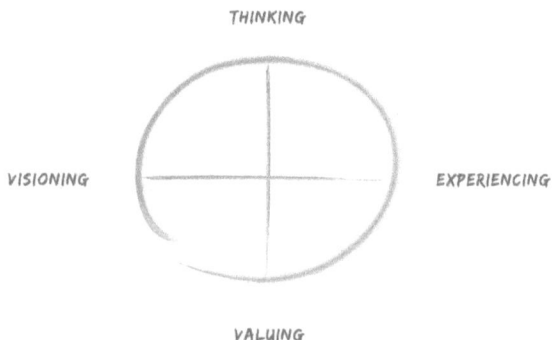

THINKING

VISIONING

EXPERIENCING

VALUING

Fig. 39:   Four complementary accesses to Reality
(Typology of C.G.Jung)

If there is enough learning in these two modes this works quite well for a long time and may lead to the conclusion, to always improve access to reality by further developing these two functions. But as always in the psychology of C.G. Jung the point is not perfection but wholeness. In the long run, the other two approaches have to be given attention and be qualified in order to gain a holistic access to reality. Development means completion of modalities not perfection within modalities, even if this means encountering clumsiness in a less familiar field.

If this development is avoided, there is a growing danger that the modalities, which do not get attention and qualification, dominate the parent accesses incompetently and subversively by acting out of the background. It helps to be aware of one's less-preferred accesses and at least understand the preferred ones.

Unreflect empirical rationalists, may be more and more controlled by misleading intultions and unconscious evaluations. Who is dedicated to visions and emotional valuing in an unreflect way, may be fail because of poor thinking and neglecting empiric data?

To dialogue with one' development concerning all four accesses to reality and to realize necessary learnings helps, not to be misled, is essential for developing a mature approach to reality.

12. Sharing culture

We are not talking about the culture section or the feuilleton, but with the business pages of the newspaper (isb-slogan).

Why a chapter on culture at the end of this handbook? Simply because after the cultural approach of the isb has been described in the introduction the following chapters explaining cultural aspects should be summarized. Culture is not an object, but a way to co-ordinate and share life. Like law culture is only of interest, when living together of humans has to be regulated. These chapters specify our perspectives and approaches to professions and organizations.

Culture was always considered in all chapters, but from different perspectives. By choosing different cultural perspectives such as leadership culture, learning culture or team culture, we were able to offer more differentiated descriptions and approaches to purposely shaping culture.

12.1. Why culture?

Culture as such cannot be directly seen or measured. It influences experience and behavior like a magnet field that structures force fields. Culture is evident in many things, such as human habits, symbols, repeated events, and the pattern of reaction.

Let's look at some cultural beliefs about culture:

At first glance, you may feel that culture is a matter of the feuilleton or something "nice to have", but in fact, it is economy, science, politics, etc.

When looking closer, you find that culture is an evolutionary "software" organizing living systems and giving them their own identity. Even animals and presumably plants develop cultural principles of co-operation through adaptation to life. For example, some orca stems hunt fish, others hunt seals, others even whales of other tribes or their babies. All teach this culture to their descendants. In this individuals develop cultural behavior and identity in their worlds.

Evolution is not just egoism and the struggle for survival and privilege. Besides mutual consumption, there is much more co-operation and co-evolution than we are used to. Orcas (killer whales), for example, learn to co-operate by swimming in the formation, thus piling up a large wave that throws a seal from its ice floe. Orcas can be caring, not just in the context of breeding. It has been observed that an adult orca with disabilities survived because other orcas have repeatedly left some fish from their own hunt.

Co-operation is not limited to members of the same species. In coral reefs, co-operation between an octopus and a grouper has been observed to hunt small fish. By poses, the grouper gave the octopus hints of hiding places of small fish, which the octopus then stirred up in order to be caught by grouper. They share their prey and thus benefit both, which is worth teaching to their offspring.

"Culture comes from culture and examples set the stage". And:
"Culture is what can bring out everyone's best and connect it in

a way, that everyone is working and living better as well as gaining more competence and dignity".

These are isb slogans. The first underlines that culture is best learned by participating in it. Neither prescriptions nor regulations, but experiencing cultural examples set the stage.

The second illustrates the benefits of changing individuals and organizations through culture.

When they are positively involved in good culture, people intuitively activate positive versions of themselves that connect them to the better parts in others. There are good reasons for the plea in the introduction of this book: If you strive results, start with culture!

Under positive cultural influence people sometimes present versions of themselves previously unknown to others or even to themselves. Note that this is not achieved through teaching and working alone, but through positive culture as long it is maintained. If this positive force collapses, people may fall behind and it may be difficult to re-activate the lost culture.

12.2. What is culture?

Culture is an "container term", representing the ways we (should) live together.

Is culture descriptive or prescriptive?

When the discussion about organizational culture started years ago, there was confusion between different general approaches. One position was, "Every culture is culture. Culture can be described as such, but little intentionally changed." Another:

"Culture means higher culture. Culture should be prescribed and realized." When culture is used for description, it should help to specify and understand how the force field of culture works.

For creative people of all kinds, for managers and service providers, the impetus for dealing with culture is the intention to either shape or change it. Subsequently, the description of cultural goals and approaches to their establishment will be included.

As culture has different aspects, there are various ways to define it. Let me introduce two examples of definitions that have proved useful for the isb.

Definition 1: Culture is describing how reality is consciously and unconsciously designed – habitually or creatively by different means.

As this definition states, some contributions to culture are conscious, but most of them are unconscious i.e. without current attention or awareness of them.

Culture is enacted both habitually and unconsciously making things easy and comfortable as long the reality created meets people`s challenges and needs. However, this can cause problems or irritation if this is not the case. Then the culture needs to be analyzed and new elements should be created, inserted and behaviorally practiced until it can be used intuitively replacing the previous habits.

Definition 2: Culture is a container term for all explicit and implicit rules of description, care and creation of reality.

Here we talk about rules. Culture is first what people experience or do without conscious awareness. It is just the way you do it and it feels "natural" as long as it is not challenged either by irritating events or other cultures.

Example:

In Germany you have to turn off your mobile phone before a performance starts. Wherever this rule is implicit, you will not be reminded, but you get a negative reaction if you break the rule.

When we recently gave a choral performance in southern Italy, nobody seemed to know this rule, and we failed establishing it in advance by an explicit statement or by strong reactions to first divergences. The performance was like a funfair and culturally very different from a similar performance in Germany.

Culture cannot be developed through instructions and campaigns in the first place, but by living examples, preferably through key players. It is like learning a new dance. Instructing alone will not help much. But if preferably key players already learned how to practice the new dance, give others the opportunity of watching them dancing and participating, the whole new system of interaction can be integrated into the existing repertoire. Thus, co-ordination of all movements can be specifically learned and shared as a new cultural element much more easily.

12.3.   Organizational Culture

Culture is required for the management of complex organizations. They cannot be controlled from the start by instructions alone, because they do not have enough impact on complex interaction of individuals according to often unconscious cultural rules. But Culture is as complex and powerful as the functioning of complex organizations. Understanding and dealing with culture is essential for understanding the organizational functioning.

Organizational culture is the "personality" of a system. Like the personality of an individual, it can be experienced immediately through many forms of expressions, though it can't be defined sharply contoured. Like the personality, culture grows over time through DNA and experience.

The DNA of an organization covers all formal structures and forming or guiding principles. In biology, besides DNA, there is also genetic material that was once considered as superfluous, but has proved to be essential: epigenetics. Epigenetic programming determines the switching of DNA segments and thus on development of the organism. Epigenetics can be shaped by experience, and so next generation can epigenetically inherit experience. This creates images how individuals can inherit experience of others in previously unknown ways. Unlike in biology, founders and managers can directly shape cultural DNA and epigenetics, making cultivation an indispensable part of their responsibilities.

12.4.   Mentality of culturing

Often executives, managers and entrepreneurs come to the isb for training or consulting, aiming to learn about starting enterprises or solving problems quickly.

Of course, they sometimes need immediate help and, if possible, a reasonable amount of it will be offered and delivered. At the same time, we appeal to the simultaneously development of culturing as a basic attitude towards leadership and entrepreneurship.

Many mistakes could be avoided if those responsible could apply the wisdom gained in areas such as gardening. If we want to plant something in our quite developed garden, the first thing that comes to mind is buying a pre-cultivated plant and putting it into a prepared whole. Sometimes that works, and it works for a while until it may become a rather miserable result.

The soil around it may not have been cultivated adequately, or the plant does not fit into the location and its plant community. The new facility may not have received enough care over time. It may also have been grown too intensely under greenhouse conditions so as not to adapt to the current outdoor conditions. Decisions may have been made by an external gardener unable to understand or care for the culture in which the new plant should grow. Eventually, much of the planting will be in vain and would have been faster and more successful if more care had been taken.

In principle, culturing in society and economy does not differ from agriculture. In the beginning, you may only need to use of a "wild" grown culture that may provide enough fruit for some time. However, if you want to ensure safe and sound quantity for more people over a longer period of time, you need to optimize the culturing. Having enjoyed the initial momentum, you find that problems accumulate over time and results decrease as long as there is no proper soil maintenance for example. Subsequently, more and more efforts are needed to offset waste and stabilize processes.

As you exhaust the system, you are increasingly confronted with failures and crisis. If you continue to cling to an exploitative and growth mentality without ground care, the basis for recovery will be severely impaired. It is high time to realize that culture and soil care is a prerequisite for sustainable social and economic developments.

12.5. Change of culture

"Whether our children learn what we want to teach them, is uncertain. But it is certain that they learn from our educational behavior." (isb-slogan)

What makes it so difficult to bring about sustainable positive systematic change?

One reason is that we are unaware of the necessary effort in cultural change and misjudge the factors stabilizing the given reality. Old habits and their interaction are underestimated while content-level statements, campaign-like events, and individual enthusiasm for change are overestimated.

In order to changing the culture of a system, new elements must be introduced at many levels and in a coordinated way, integrating learning and practicing new cultural elements by involving all those who share work and responsibility in every-day life. The new culture can only be sustained if it is exercised to a degree in which it is usually stronger than the old culture. The more new cultural elements break with traditions practiced, the more carefully they need to be introduced and re-peated over and over again. To be effective, they just have to override the existing habits. In order to achieve this easier, new cultural element should be built on traditions and their value background in order to avoiding loyalty problems.

When a new business comes into play or cultural issues need to be resolved immediately, the scope for an accepted and intended culture may be tight. This can lead to an attempt to start with a low cultural level, hoping to improve culture later. Here the organization gets on the wrong track, as it is the beginning in which the cultural character is imprinted. Having accepted an inadequate lamp in your living room once, it takes an extra effort changing it later. Each system tends to preserve and develop all, that was originally in place. Once these imprints become unconscious and are reenacted through the interplay of many players, it becomes very difficult to identify and change them.

A basis for successful cultural change is a realistic assessment of starting conditions, i.e. maturity and resources available, such as motivation, time, energy support, etc. The other basic factor is the creation and control of the change process over a sufficient period of time.

Fostering the necessary investment and expertise for cultural change is an essential and increasingly relevant part of leadership. Responsibility usually has to be met internally, a requirement that does not need to be replaced by major events and expensive services through external consultants.

The size of the challenge depends on the ability to develop of individuals, teams, the organization as a whole, and sometimes the environment in which the organization is engaged.

13. Instructions for further work on the isb campus

German Version: www.isb-handbuch.eu
German and English version are identical.

There are two versions of the isb-manual on isb-campus:

- Complete version with the table of contents.

- Overview about the single chapters according to their topics. The tables of contents for each of these chapters correspond to the count in the complete version.

Further references and materials for in-depth study of each chapter are placed on the isb campus in public watch lists (overview about all note lists).

There you will find references to in-depth study opportunities and links to the free available writings, audios, videos and charts.

For many of the topics there are "click to transfer" versions. Here you can browse PowerPoint charts and click to dive directly into the corresponding video sequences. You can download the charts individually or as a package and use them with your own logo. In addition, there is didactic material for many topics, such as handouts, exercises and designs, which you can also reuse. A free registration is necessary for this.

So are available:

- The complete version with table of content

- Overview of diagrams (by chapters and numbering according to complete version)

- Bullet point lists from the complete version (ordered according chapters)

- Single chapters with respective active tables of contents (all numbering according to the complete text) and

- Links to watch lists on campus with all in-depth material.

In the digital version
www.isb-w.eu/campus/de/themenkoerbe/isb_handbook.php
you will find all direct links to these offers in this user guide.

www.youtube.com/user/ISBlearning

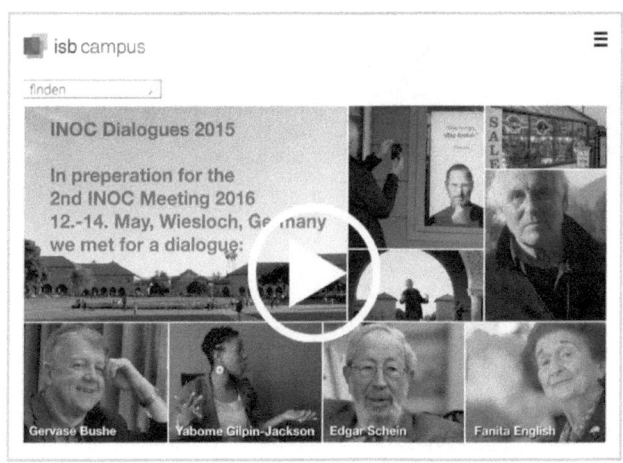

www.isb-w.eu/
campus/de/themenkoerbe/tc_inoc_dialogues_campus.php

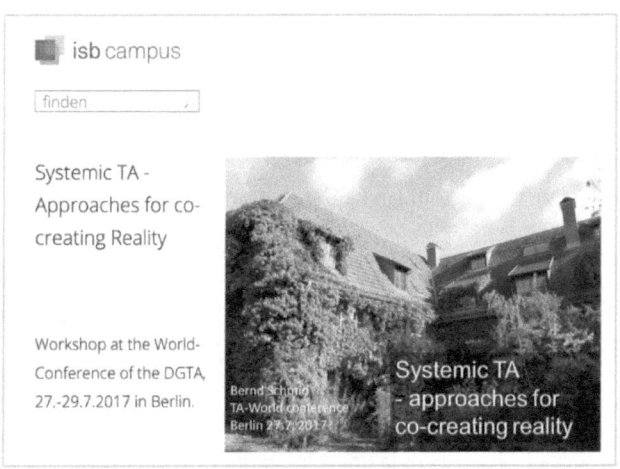

www.isb-w.eu/campus/de/themenkoerbe/transactional_analysis.php

B. Schmid / A. Geethan: Guided Journey of a Caterpillar.
A transition from personal orientation to Organizational Development
- free download isb-campus.

This book is on attitudes, ideas, concepts and approaches around building up an internal learning culture with the help of organizational coaches. Organizational Coaching in general improves relationships between human beings and the organizations they work for. Building a learning culture means to connect learning behaviors of individuals and groups of people with learning programs to gain adequate competence and finally reach desired performance.

Zeitfracht Medien GmbH
Ferdinand-Jühlke-Straße 7
99095 Erfurt, Deutschland
produktsicherheit@kolibri360.de